SOCIAL HEALTH INSURANCE

International Labour Office - Geneva   International Social Security Association

Copyright © International Labour Organization 1997

Publications of the International Labour Office enjoy copyright under Protocol 2 of the Universal Copyright Convention. Nevertheless, short excerpts from them may be reproduced without authorization, on condition that the source is indicated. For rights of reproduction or translation, application should be made to the Publications Bureau (Rights and Permissions), International Labour Office, CH-1211 Geneva 22, Switzerland. The International Labour Office welcomes such applications.

Libraries, institutions and other users registered in the United Kingdom with the Copyright Licensing Agency, 90 Tottenham Court Road, London W1P 9HE (Fax: + 44 171 436 3986), in the United States with the Copyright Clearance Center, 222 Rosewood Drive, Danvers, MA 01923 (Fax: + 1 508 750 4470) or in other countries with associated Reproduction Rights Organizations, may make photocopies in accordance with the licences issued to them for this purpose.

First published 1999

ISBN 92-2-110738-8

The designations employed in ILO publications, which are in conformity with United Nations practice, and the presentation of material therein do not imply the expression of any opinion whatsoever on the part of the International Labour Office concerning the legal status of any country, area or territory or of its authorities, or concerning the delimitation of its frontiers.

The responsibility for opinions expressed in signed articles, studies and other contributions rests solely with their authors, and publication does not constitute an endorsement by the International Labour Office of the opinions expressed in them.

Reference to names of firms and commercial products and processes does not imply their endorsement by the International Labour Office, and any failure to mention a particular firm, commercial product or process is not a sign of disapproval.

ILO publications can be obtained through major booksellers or ILO local offices in many countries, or direct from ILO Publications, International Labour Office, CH-1211 Geneva 22, Switzerland. A catalogue or list of new publications will be sent free of charge from the above address.

Author unit: SEC/SOC
Editor: T. Whitaker
Designer: P. Bissaca, E. Fortarezza
Production: International Training Centre of the ILO, Turin, Italy

PREFACE

This manual is one of a series produced by the Social Security Department of the International Labour Office (ILO), Geneva, in cooperation with the International Social Security Association (ISSA) and the International Training Centre of the International Labour Organization, Turin.

The manual examines the main elements of social health insurance and draws attention to some of the choices for financing and managing health care.

Other publications in the series:
- Social Security Principles
- Administration of Social Security
- Pension Schemes
- Social Security Financing
- Trainers Guide

The manuals have been produced primarily for use in countries where social security systems are not yet operational, are undergoing change or need to be improved. In particular, the manuals will be useful in developing countries, countries in transition, and countries undergoing structural change, as they begin the process of setting up new systems of social protection or of improving existing systems.

It should be noted, however, that the information contained in this manual – in common with others in the series – refers almost entirely to the formal sector and not to the wide range of systems which apply to groups outside the traditional social security system.

It will be appreciated that, in a manual of this size, it is possible to provide only a broad overview of the topic. For the reader needing more extensive or detailed information about social health insurance, there may well be a need for additional reading. Publications dealing with various aspects of health insurance are numerous and several are referred to in the further reading list at the end of the manual.

It is important to make clear to readers of the manual that no attempt is made within these pages to provide a description of a Astandard model" of social health insurance for, as should become clear on reading the manual, there is no such thing !

Thanks are due to Ms. Monica Burns (late of the ILO Social Security Department) who produced the initial draft, to Dr. Aviva Ron (ILO Health Insurance specialist) and Dr. Axel

Weber (ILO consultant) who both made significant and substantial revisions to the original text, and to all those people – too many to mention individually – who have helped in some way in the preparation of this manual. It should also be acknowledged that substantial use has been made of an earlier ILO publication – *HEALTH INSURANCE IN DEVELOPING COUNTRIES* – and of a publication jointly produced by WHO and ILO – *SOCIAL HEALTH INSURANCE, A GUIDEBOOK FOR PLANNING* – both of which are included in the Further Reading section at the end of the manual.

Readers who are more interested in quantitative techniques in health care financing might also be interested to see the recent publication – *"Modelling in health care financing"* – produced jointly by ILO/ISSA in the series on *"Quantitative techniques in social protection"*.

Should any reader wish to offer comment or feedback on the contents of this or any other manual in the series, please write to:

> The International Labour Office
> SEC SOC, 9th Floor
> 4 route des Morillons
> CH-1211 Genève 22
> Switzerland
> Fax (+41.22) 799.7962

> # TABLE OF CONTENTS

		Page
Module 1	**Health care policy and social health insurance**	**1**
	Introduction	5
	Unit 1 Social health insurance as part of health care policy	9
	Unit 2 Feasibility issues	22
	Unit 3 Issues for planning	30
Module 2	**Designing a social health insurance scheme**	**33**
	Introduction	37
	Unit 1 Coverage	38
	Unit 2 The health care benefits	47
Module 3	**Providing the health care benefits**	**59**
	Unit 1 Who will be the partners?	63
	Unit 2 Provider contracts	71
	Unit 3 Accreditation of providers and Quality Assurance	74
	Unit 4 Choice of provider for the insured	80
Module 4	**Financing social health insurance**	**83**
	Unit 1 Contributions	87
	Unit 2 Other sources of financing	92
Module 5	**Provider payment**	**95**
	Unit 1 Provider payment mechanisms	99
	Unit 2 Issues to consider	106

Module 6	**The insurance organization**	**111**
	Unit 1 Organizational aspects	115
	Unit 2 Contact with other agencies	131
Module 7	**Information systems**	**135**
	Unit 1 .Internal information	139
	Unit 2 External information	144
Module 8	**A Primer on Micro-Insurance**	**147**
	Unit 1 What is *Micro-Insurance?*	151
	Unit 2 Main features	155
	Unit 3 Micro-Insurance as an alternative	158

Epilogue	**161**
Further reading	**163**
New literature	166

SOCIAL HEALTH INSURANCE

MODULE 1:
HEALTH CARE POLICY
AND
SOCIAL HEALTH INSURANCE

International Labour Office　　　　　　International Social Security Association

MODULE CONTENTS

Introduction

Unit 1   Social health insurance as part of health care policy

    A.   The concept of social health insurance

    B.   Solidarity and equity issues related to social health insurance

    C.   Alternative concepts of financing health care services

    D.   Why introduce social health insurance?

Unit 2   Feasibility issues

    A.   Cultural and traditional considerations

    B.   Equity

    C.   The labour market

    D.   Administrative implications

    E.   The health care infrastructure

Unit 3   Issues for planning

MODULE 1

HEALTH CARE POLICY AND SOCIAL HEALTH INSURANCE

Introduction

The first of the manuals in this series – *Social Security Principles*[1] – set out the background to and historical development of **social security** which is the term used to refer to ...

...the protection which society provides for its members ... through a series of public measures ... against the economic and social distress that would otherwise be caused by the stoppage or substantial reduction of earnings ... resulting from sickness, maternity, employment injury, unemployment, invalidity, old age and death; ... **the provision of medical care***, ... and the provision of subsidies for families with children ...A*

All the risks referred to, for which conventional social security is designed, are in some way related to health. In the case of employment injury, sickness, invalidity, disablement and maternity, they are directly related; in the case of old age pensions, survivor's pensions, family benefit and unemployment benefit they are indirectly related since these benefits are intended to maintain the beneficiaries in a state of adequate nutrition and good health.

The connection between ill-health and poverty, with each often being a principal cause of the other, does not need to be emphasized. Perhaps it is therefore not surprising that medical care is the first of the social security benefits listed in the Social Security (Minimum Standards) Convention, 1952 (No.102)[2]. The Convention establishes that medical care benefit is provided with a view to maintaining, restoring or improving

---

1 *Social Security Principles* – (Manual No.1 in this series) – Social Security Department, ILO Geneva, 1998. ISBN92-2-110734-5
2 ILO Conventions and Recommendations are fully explained in the Manual *Social Security Principles* (Module 6)

the health of those protected and their ability to work and to attend to personal needs. The Convention also establishes the minimum content of health care benefit as:

- general practitioner care, including home visits;
- specialist care in hospitals and similar institutions for in-patients and out-patients and such specialist care as may be available outside hospitals;
- essential pharmaceutical supplies;
- pre-natal, confinement and post-natal care by medical practitioners or qualified midwives and
- hospitalization where necessary.

To this list the Medical Care and Sickness Benefits Convention, 1969 (No.130) adds:

- dental care and
- medical rehabilitation, including necessary appliances.

Convention 102 does not require that this *full* range of health care is available to the *whole* population, indeed the Convention's requirements are satisfied if 50 per cent of employees, 20 per cent of the economically active population, or 50 per cent of residents are covered. However, it is generally recognized – and is established in ILO Recommendation No.69: Medical Care, 1944 – that the State has the overall responsibility for creating a medical care service for *all* persons, whether or not they are gainfully employed, with a view to:

a) restoring health (providing curative care), and

b) protecting and improving health (providing preventive care).

As shown by broad international experience, the underlying threats to good health are well known and affordable solutions are frequently available but, because of weak government implementation capacity and market imperfections in the private sector, potentially effective policies and programmes often fail.

Most countries have realized that the responsibilities for providing health care cannot be wholly fulfilled by reliance on market forces and that some form of direct involvement by the State is essential in order to ensure that the potentially monopolistic power of providers does not work against the interests of consumers and patients, many of whom may be ignorant or uncertain both of health matters and of their entitlements.

Today, in low-income countries – where public revenues are scarce and institutional capacity in the public sector is weak – the financing and delivery of health, nutrition and population services is largely in the private sector. In many of those countries, large segments of the poor still have no access to basic or effective care for a variety of reasons.

Fig. 1:
"... large segments of the poor ... have no access ... to ... basic ... care ..."

In most developed countries – and in many middle-income countries – governments have become central to social policy and health care. This involvement by the public sector is justified both on theoretical and practical grounds to improve

- equity – by securing access by the population to health, nutrition, and reproductive services

and

- efficiency – by correcting for market failures.

Private voluntary health insurance is an area which is sometimes prone to market imperfections. While insurance may succeed in protecting people against selected risks, it sometimes excludes those who need health insurance the most or who are at the greatest risk of illness. Private insurers may also have an incentive to exclude costly medical conditions or to minimize their financial risk through the use of benefit caps and exclusions. The result can be to limit protection against the most expensive and catastrophic illnesses.

Some of the actions taken by governments to correct market failures – ranging from the least to the greatest intervention – include:

- providing information to encourage behaviour changes needed for long-term improvements in health, nutrition, and population outcomes;

- enforcing regulations and incentives to influence public and private sector activities;
- issuing mandates to indirectly finance or provide services;
- financing or providing subsidies to pay for services or influence prices; and
- direct public production of preventative and curative health services.

Economic principles and empirical evidence both suggest that a mixture of public and private involvement leads to the best results. Neither sector is totally effective by itself – each needs the other. Both too much and too little involvement by either sector often leads to problems.

Government intervention, however, implies the need for a *health policy*. While this may be expressed in terms of "measures to protect people from avoidable disease and to provide efficient health services", a number of policy decisions will need to be taken with regard to the allocation of resources to, and within, the health sector (to reflect choices as to priorities) and also with regard to those aspects which should be financed by the State and those which should be left to individual responsibility.

The national health policy which is adopted will depend on the economic, historic and cultural context and, in particular, will reflect the stage of development of – and the interaction with – other policy objectives. But government resources will rarely be sufficient to meet *all* heath care demands and they should not therefore be used to subsidize health care which is inconsistent with or does not contribute to health policy objectives.

UNIT 1: Social health insurance as part of health care policy

A. The concept of social health insurance

Social health insurance and private insurance both represent mechanisms which enable the burden of the direct cost of medical care for the patient to be spread:

- either – over a period of time rather than having to be made at the time and point of delivery
- and/or among a group of people who share the risk of costs of medical care.

Fig. 2:
"... mechanisms ... enable the burden of cost ... to be spread ... over ... time ... or among a group ..."

Since social health insurance requires the establishment, under statute, of a social insurance fund (based on the contributions of employers, insured persons and perhaps also government) it can also lead to the identification and collection of additional government resources which may be allocated in a way that is consistent with health policy objectives. In this way the costs of medical care are spread among an even larger group, perhaps even among all tax payers.

The linkage between the contributions of employers and insured persons and the health care entitlement of the latter introduces a greater measure of control and monitoring in the system and should lead to increased accountability, especially as employers are interested in achieving lower wage costs.

The term *social health insurance* is used to describe a method of financing and managing health care

- which depends for its resources on compulsory contributions from employers and employees, and perhaps also from government,

- where individual health risks (pre-existing conditions, age, disability etc.) do *not* influence the level of contributions or do not inevitably lead to exclusions from protection,

- where contributions are often based on ability to pay and

- which is a non-profit concept.

Social health insurance, by definition, is based on the concept of pooling of risks and resources. It is a financially viable option *only* if the health risk factors associated with the membership group are balanced by the income from contributions or from government transfers.

In *private* health insurance schemes the risks – both health and occupational – are borne by the individual. There are various ways in which private health insurance schemes control the risk-mix and the financial equilibrium of the scheme, for example:

- the premiums are mostly set on an individual basis, which means that the level of the premium is influenced by age and sex,

- pre-existing diseases or disabilities may influence the level of premiums,

- qualifying periods are applied to all new contracts,

- exclusion of individuals with pre-existing conditions or with disabilities is a common instrument of private insurance schemes,

- it is the practice in many countries to cancel the insurance contract at the onset of a chronic disease or when insured members have made expensive claims.

These practices are common because they are a way of protecting the insurance scheme from adverse risk selection. Normally *private* insurances are based on *voluntary* membership and are thus vulnerable to such phenomena. The consequence of this practice is that people with health risks, and those who cannot afford the risk-related premium, are excluded from solidarity mechanisms.

Finally, it should also be remembered that the main difference from social insurance is that most private schemes are commercially based and thus profit motivated, as are other voluntary non-government schemes. This involves a cost factor which also influences the level of premiums.

In a *social* health insurance scheme, the balance of risks is normally achieved by mechanisms which are different to those in private insurance, for example:

- in most cases membership is compulsory and this results in a mix of risks of the target group covered.

    Healthy and sick, wealthy and poor, are all members of the insurance scheme and there is no chance to practice an adverse risk selection. *Compulsory* membership is normally an instrument which is reserved for *social* health insurance schemes.

- if compulsory membership is not achieved, other mechanisms (e.g. social marketing, qualifying periods, or control in small community groups) may help to prevent adverse risk selection and, at the same time, maintain the features of social health insurance, especially the non-exclusion of risks and bearable contributions.

Social health insurance also differs from private health insurance in the *liability* of the individual. Under a social health insurance scheme, individuals make either a flat-rate payment or an earnings-related payment, i.e. the level of payment is not in any way related to the individual's health risk, or to diseases or symptoms previously presented by the individual, or to chronic diseases suffered by the individual. The concept of "paying according to means and using according to need" becomes a basic principle. Many social health insurance schemes cover not only the individual who pays the contributions but also that individual's family members.

Social health insurance thus embodies a strong social purpose, unlike private-for-profit or commercial health insurance where individual risk is the basis used by the insurer to set the level of the premium. For this reason *social insurance* is the term used to describe *health insurance* programmes based on social solidarity with the emphasis more on *"social"* than on *"insurance"*.

Another special feature of social health insurance is the legal environment. Normally social health insurance is based on legal provisions which are quite different from private health insurance and prices, fees, contracts with providers, benefits and health objectives, are all regulated by law and thus are of public interest and under public control. The fact that many social health insurance schemes are based on compulsory contributions explains this greater level of standardization and monitoring. This should result in a greater level of consumer protection.

Social health insurance schemes are *non-profit* organizations. This means that they have no shareholders or private owners to satisfy and they therefore have lower costs. On the other hand, however, this means that social health insurance schemes have no possibility of generating capital through the issue of shares or by any other kind of private investment. All the necessary capital has to be accumulated – either from contributions (saving), or by bank or State credits, or by transfers from the State budget. This causes a problem of liquidity, especially in the initial phase of a social health insurance scheme when there is a need for investment capital but still insufficient income from contributions.

The issue of *compulsory* and *voluntary* insurance should not be confused with *social* and private insurance. When the payment of contributions to a social health insurance scheme is mandated by legislation or by government decree, the term *compulsory insurance* is applied. When the payment of insurance premiums is left to the discretion of individuals, whether in social insurance schemes or in non-government or private schemes, the term *voluntary health insurance* is used. Nevertheless, the *mandatory* membership is mostly a feature reserved for *social* health insurance schemes.

B. Solidarity and equity issues related to social health insurance

Equity considerations have influenced thinking about access to health care for many years. Equity, in the context of social health insurance, means the guaranteed access of the whole population of a country to a package of health services by paying an affordable contribution or (for some groups) no contribution at all.

However, there may be reasons why the objective of covering the whole population is difficult to achieve, for example:

- if the scheme is the first stage in a longer-term policy development, it *may* be acceptable to have a period in which equity objectives are deliberately not met;

- it may be difficult – for technical reasons – to cover the whole population (e.g. lack of infrastructure, large differences in income and education, no formalized employment etc.) and registration and contribution collection procedures, especially, may create difficulties;

- the available funds to develop the insurance scheme for the country may be too small;
- there may be too much resistance among the better-off section of the population, or those in formalized employments, to participate in a system which is built on solidarity with the poor. In some countries there is still no support for such a concept and acceptance of the concept needs to be promoted step by step. Meanwhile "second best" solutions must be found for the vulnerable part of the population.

A population's desire for access to health services stems from a comparison with similar populations within and beyond the country; providing services for only one section of the population may also be seen as depriving others, especially if government resources are used to create or run the scheme.

On the other hand, if health insurance releases government resources to develop services for people not covered by the scheme – and thus raises standards for the people who are worst off – greater inequality may be acceptable.

One of the key tenets of a social health insurance system is the concept of *social solidarity*. Social solidarity comes about from the obligation of some people to pay *more* than is required to cover their own risks while, at the same time, accepting that there will always be others paying *less* than is required to cover their risks. This solidarity can be practised within a social insurance scheme or through tax-financed services for the poorer section of the population, though the standard of health care may not be the same.

Fig. 3:
"One of the key tenets of ... Social health insurance ... is social solidarity."

Permitting *voluntary* membership of a scheme brings with it the problem that the ones who *choose* to join tend to be those with the highest risks and fewest resources and this "adverse selection" results in a much higher per capita cost. Where membership is *compulsory*, however, good and bad risks are pooled, resources are shared, and thus the financial viability of the arrangement is much greater, with each individual member expecting to receive – as of right – the medical care which is needed in return for a contribution which is affordable.

The introduction of social health insurance can improve access to medical care for some groups as well as providing additional resources for the health sector as a whole. In principle, a social health insurance scheme which covers, for example, only formal sector workers can free resources from the public health budget. Those resources can then be devoted, for example, to the improvement or extension of primary care facilities in rural areas. In this case, the total resources for health care in the country would increase and more health care facilities and/or better quality would thus be affordable. The condition is, however, that the government does *not* withdraw the freed resources after the introduction of health insurance.

There are some dangers here, for example that the introduction of social health insurance, at least for a transitional period, may result in problems of health care provision and thus produce a limitation to equity. The additional demands of those covered under the social health insurance scheme may require the allocation of scarce resources – such as medical staff, drugs and hospital beds.

Nevertheless, it should be remembered that operating a social health insurance scheme is a dynamic process and, although initially there may well be some limitations, it is likely that this will be followed by later expansion and an improvement in equity in access to health care.

Social health insurance creates a commitment to ensure access to health care services and that commitment must be matched by an acceptable level of supply. In many developing countries there is a severe shortage of trained medical staff and suitable infrastructure and although, to some extent, the additional resources provided by the scheme could be expected to help in the alleviation of this problem, insured persons will expect an immediate improvement in the quality of medical care.

C. Alternative concepts of financing health care services

Issues to consider

The issues to be considered which are specifically related to finance are:

- what are the methods of financing?
- what are the sources of finance?

Methods of financing

There are four main methods of financing health services:

- financing by public budget
- financing by social health insurance
- financing by private insurance
- financing by direct payment by patients.

Each of these methods impacts differently on the accessibility of health care, on health care provision and its prices, and of course on distribution of health care costs among the users.

The question of the method of financing is also related to the question of ownership of and responsibility for the facilities providing health care -

- The State may act as the provider, either directly through a public health care system or
- indirectly, through a parastatal organization established by statute.
- NGOs and other private non-profit-making organizations may provide, as may
- private profit-making organizations.

Returning to the four methods of financing, the State may provide services free at the point of delivery on a universal basis. However, in many countries where this system has been adopted it has not proved possible to allocate sufficient resources to meet the increasing demand for health care. Consequently, in practice, coverage has often been limited, both in the quality of the service provided and in its accessibility. This has been reflected in lower health care standards and, in turn, has obliged many countries to seek alternative or supplementary sources of health care financing under which the contribution by the patient is more directly linked to the health care provided – which also exercises some restraint on demand.

At the other end of the spectrum from *free* public health care systems are those where the patient *pays directly* for the health care provided by a private hospital, clinic or general practitioner. The patient may *choose* to pay – despite the existence of a public health care system – because of dissatisfaction with the level of care provided by that system. Direct payment, by the patient (or by the employer) at the point of delivery may also apply in the case of a public health care system where it has been decided that there is either a need to increase resources or to control costs through the introduction of a cost sharing element or user fee.

As an alternative to public health care provision and payment by the patient is insurance and there are two options:

- private insurance

    and

- social insurance.

The differences between the two concepts were explained earlier and it is *social insurance* which will be the main focus of the manual.

Fig. 4:
"... Social insurance ... the main focus of the manual ..."

Different concepts of health care financing

Concept	Distributive effects	Access to health care	Influence on provision	Problems
State budget	Financed by all tax payers	Everybody	Often own facilities. Control of costs and quality possible	Limitation of State funds
Social health insurance	Financed by employers and employees, sometimes by State subsidies. Contributions not risk related. Contributions according ability to pay. Sometimes co-payments	Insured only. No exclusion of disabled and sick	Often own facilities or contracted facilities. Control of prices and quality possible	Registration and contribution payment of informal sector. Evasion
Private insurance	Contributions risk related. No social elements. Higher contributions in the case of existing diseases.	Insured only. Exclusion of bad risks	Often very low influence due to limited market position. No negotiation of prices but reimbursement. Exception: HMOs	For the majority of the population too expensive. Problems for sick and disabled
Individual payment	Only the sick and their families pay. The healthy have no costs at all	Only those who can pay have access	No control of prices or quality	High economic risk, or no health care especially for the poorer population

The financing of social health insurance is related to and affected by a number of issues – the range of benefits, population coverage, cost control and, of course, the sources of finance.

Sources of finance

There are a number of potential sources of finance:

- ***Government subsidies*** and ***tax relief*** which include

    - subsidies or budget guarantees to cover deficits;
    - subsidies to cover health costs of certain groups (including for example, military personnel, civil servants, etc., as well as some non-contributory groups – the handicapped, prisoners, etc., – and perhaps also people undertaking activities which are exempt from taxation);
    - subsidies to cover the contributions of certain groups;
    - subsidies to cover certain investment costs in order to influence resource allocation;
    - general subsidies, covering a certain percentage or a fixed; – amount of the overall costs;
    - subsidies to cover the cost of certain services provided by social health insurance;
    - subsidies to cover the administration of the scheme, for example by paying the salary of the staff;
    - deduction of contributions to social health insurance from taxable income;
    - exemption of health insurance from certain taxes like company taxes, property taxes, insurance taxes, VAT etc..

- ***Contributions*** – which may be

    - flat-rate and equal;
    - wage related (percentage of wage or according to classes of wages, with or without an upper limit);
    - income related (taking account of total income – not only wages);
    - related to regions (different contribution classes from region to region).

(Note that the four contribution systems referred to are listed in order of complexity and administrative difficulty)

These contributions may be payable monthly, semestrally, every six months or yearly.

- ***Co-payments***

    These may exist for example as a percentage of the costs or prices, as a flat rate per service, per contact with a facility or per product (drug). Co-payments may exempt certain vulnerable groups.

- *User charges*

    (which are a special form of co-payment) like fees for consultations, fees per diem in hospitals, neither of which are intended to cover the total costs.

- *Consumer taxes*

    which are used by some countries (e.g. France) with the objectives of discouraging people from engaging in hazardous activities or behaviour, and of covering the costs incurred by the health fund, which result. Examples include tobacco and alcohol consumption, traffic accidents and hazardous sports, all of which place direct or indirect demands on health services.

- *Interest on reserves*

    many health funds are obliged – and most others choose – to hold reserves, and the amount of interest produced by those reserves depends on the quality of the fund's financial management. That interest may form a source of income for a health fund.

- *Other sources of income*

    although they may only represent a small part of the income of the health fund, examples of other sources are:

    - fines for late payment (e.g. of health insurance contributions);
    - payments for services provided on behalf of other authorities;
    - indemnities (e.g. those paid by other insurance organizations in respect of victims of traffic accidents);
    - revenue from the provision of services, in facilities owned and operated by the fund, to non-members;
    - revenue from the sale of goods and services by the health fund to members.

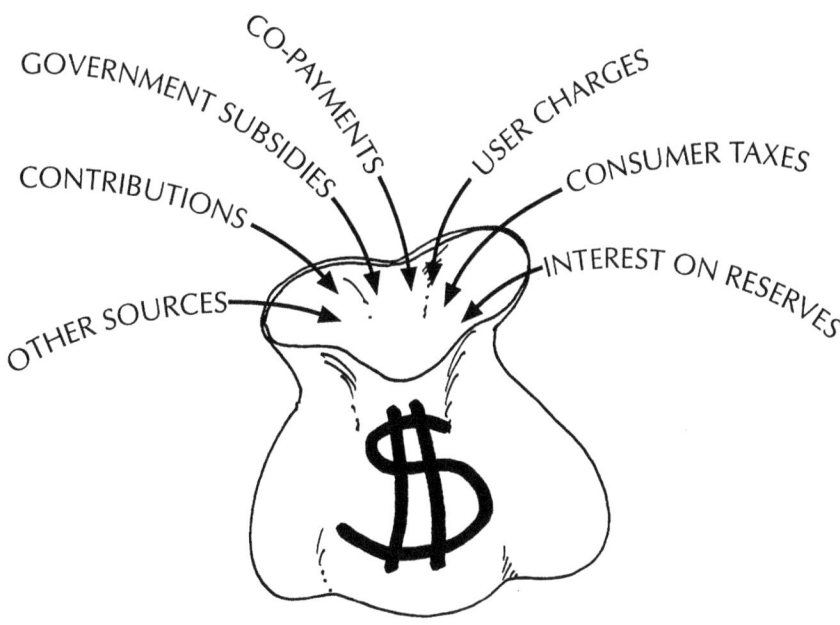

Fig. 5:
"... a number of potential sources of finance ..."

D. Why introduce social health insurance?

Social health insurance has several features which make it attractive as a policy alternative:

- it can provide additional resources to cover the needs of the population;

- it is a subsidiary way to provide and manage health care services and an alternative to increasing State responsibilities;

- it is an element of consumer protection because it may have influences on the prices and the quality of health care providers via contracts;

- it allows a separation of financing and health care provision; (Providers and financing institutions may be partners with separate interests, which may lead to better control and better quality);

- it makes all the concerned partners (the insured, employers and providers) more aware of costs. In particular, the influence of employers may lead to more efficient measures of cost control.

The priority given to health care increases as a country gets richer. Poorer countries typically spend about 3 to 4 per cent of their national income on health care with richer countries spending about 8 to 10 per cent. To some extent, this reflects the greater priority accorded to basic infrastructure which may contribute indirectly, but significantly, to health standards and reinforce general accessibility.

Social health insurance may provide a mechanism for making additional resources available but it does not, in itself, make it possible for a country to afford all the health care needed. It can, however, close the gap between what a country can afford and the resources which can be mobilized through the tax system or through private insurance. In this context, the desirability of the introduction of social health insurance should be considered with regard to the following -

- Is the development of health care inhibited by disparities and inefficiencies in allocation, rather than by limited resources?

- Is the growth of the economy sufficiently strong and durable to permit a further development of health services?

- Would the introduction of social health insurance increase the efficiency of the use of resources?

- Would the introduction of health insurance supplement or replace existing financial contributions?
- Would the State direct resources towards more vulnerable groups?
- Finally, will the introduction of health insurance be technically feasible in the existing environment?

Unit 2: Feasibility issues

Introduction

Besides assessing the affordability of services and the potential role of insurance, it is important to look at the *feasibility* of social health insurance. Among other things, it is necessary to identify the administrative needs of an insurance system and decide whether they can be met. Insurance arrangements tend to be more complex – and often more expensive to administer – than tax funding and certainly require considerable administrative skills. There are a number of other aspects which will affect the overall feasibility of introducing a social health insurance scheme and some of these are discussed in the following sections.

A. Cultural and traditional considerations

Introduction of a social health insurance scheme will inevitably be against a background of existing attitudes and traditions in health service provision. There may be some resistance to the new concept both by providers and by those who are insured.

If health care has previously been provided free at the point of use, through a public system financed by taxes, there may well be a resistance to changing to a system where payment is more visible and, particularly, a resistance to the *requirement* to contribute. On the other hand, what was an *apparently* free system may, in practice, also have involved "unofficial payments" to medical staff, by those needing medical treatment, in order to ensure priority treatment or to obtain a better level of care.

Where such practices do exist, providers may be reluctant to see such arrangements replaced by health insurance, particularly if this is likely to reduce the opportunities to maintain their incomes, perhaps more than half of which may come from such unofficial payments.

Bearing in mind that social health insurance is based on mutual support – involving the transfer of resources from those who have *higher* incomes to those who have *lower* incomes – it works bes*t* when there is a consensus among the population that mutual support *is* a good thing. It will be very difficult to promote acceptance of a scheme if there is no such consensus! It should also be remembered that it has been shown that "richer" people may have more health problems involving higher costs, e.g. heart disease. Moreover, especially in rural areas, the infrastructure of health facilities is much worse than in urban areas. This may produce the effect that transfers from richer to poorer people are less than they may appear.

The regular payment of contributions may be a concept which is not understood by many individuals, especially in developing countries. People wonder why they should pay if they are not ill. The concept of insurance must therefore be explained and promoted.

The actual payment of the contribution sometimes causes problems, especially when, for example, neither individuals nor employers have bank accounts and live in remote areas. In these cases, technical alternatives have to be developed, for example co-operation with post offices, with public administration, with health care facilities, etc..

Insurance brings with it a different relationship between physician and patient – a "customer/service-provider relationship" – which may conflict with tradition because the health insurance scheme effectively becomes a "third party" involved in the pricing of, payment for, and quality control of, services and this may be perceived as limiting professional freedom. On the other hand, providers in most countries where health insurance has been introduced like the financial reliability and the increase in demand which it creates.

One other factor also needs to be borne in mind. Social health insurance is usually financed by payroll contributions, shared between employer and worker. A prescribed percentage is deducted, by the employer, from the employee's salary; that amount – together with the employer's contribution – is then paid (by the employer) to the social health insurance fund. In most countries similar arrangements are already in force as a means of financing *other* social insurance benefits or taxes. Any increase in the overall rate of deductions may well be resisted by employers (who are likely to see this as an increase in labour costs) *and* by workers (for whom it will result in a reduced level of take-home pay).

In most countries, the payroll is already a major source of taxation – pension and other social security benefit contributions, income tax, unemployment insurance and, sometimes, insurance payments against ill-health and consequential loss of earnings, etc. If these deductions are already high then it may be a problem to use the payroll as the source of additional contributions – for health insurance.

Further payroll charges may discourage employers from retaining or recruiting staff – which leads to higher unemployment. It is possible that there will be less resistance to an increase in the payroll deductions if the introduction of the health insurance contribution coincides with a planned increase in salaries.

Despite such difficulties, the payroll source probably provides the most efficient method of collection and it may also serve to increase compliance with the requirement to pay contributions for other social security benefits. Health care is the most frequently used social security benefit and therefore failure to pay contributions creates more frequent problems than, for example, for retirement benefits.

B. Equity

Attempts to obtain the objective of equity of access to health care services in many developing countries will encounter the problem that the infrastructure of health care facilities is much less developed in rural areas than in urban and that, within the same country, there may be enormous differences in the possibilities for providing care. Removing such differences is rarely possible taking into account the fact that

- in some countries 80% of the population lives in rural areas, where the per capita income is less than 30% of that in urban areas;

- the distance from villages to the next small or medium town may be quite far;

- tertiary or even secondary care facilities only make sense if the population covered is large enough;

- the resources, even after the introduction of health insurance, will not be large enough to cover the country with facilities of the same level.

Thus, for the same contribution rate, the quality and level of care provided will be very different. This is why, in some countries, contributions are different from region to region.

On the other hand, the introduction of social health insurance can provide improved access for some groups of the population and may widen coverage by bringing additional resources into the health sector. Funds which are released – by moving part of the population from a government-funded to a social insurance-funded system of care – can allow other priority services to be developed. For example, resources thus freed up can be used

- to improve the provision of services to population sub-groups which are not covered by the social health insurance scheme

and

- to improve public health services.

C. The labour market

The formal and informal sectors

Although many countries have devised ways of doing so with varying levels of success, it is difficult to administer a social insurance scheme in respect of members of the labour force who have low or irregular incomes and who either work on their own account or do not work on the basis of a regular and continuing employer/employee relationship. Not only is it difficult to identify and register such persons but it is also difficult to accurately determine their incomes – and therefore to collect the appropriate contributions. Furthermore, where there is no employer, a means must be found of devising a contribution rate which does not prejudice the solidarity basis of the scheme.

For these reasons it is often decided, in developing a social insurance scheme, to begin the application of the scheme with formal sector employees – in respect of whom the administrative implications are more straightforward. If, however, the formal sector represents only a small section of the labour force, then consideration will be needed as to whether priority should be given to establishing a social health insurance scheme *only* for them, or to developing an alternative system which could embrace the informal sector *and* the self-employed, or of giving priority to improving health care services (such as primary care) which would benefit the population as a whole.

Structure of the labour market

A further factor to consider is the *structure* of the labour market. There may be a trend, in countries which are going through economic transition, for the proportion of the population in formal employment to fall and for more people to become self-employed.

It is difficult to assess the income of the self-employed because

- income throughout the year tends to fluctuate and vary,
- business and personal incomes are often confused,

- and the self-employed often attempt to understate their income to avoid or reduce tax payments.

Social health insurance contributions are usually set at a *fixed* percentage of income, which implies there being an agreed and easily identifiable *measure* of income. For the reasons given above, it is often difficult to make that identification for a self-employed worker.

Social health insurance therefore works best in the context of a *formal* sector, where a large proportion of the workforce are working as salaried employees and for whom there is little doubt about their income level – and therefore about the contribution required from them.

The self-employed

Despite the problems referred to earlier, it *is* nevertheless possible to operate schemes for the self-employed and for the informal sector and there are many ways of assessing the level of contribution required. For example

- where incomes are consistently understated, a higher contribution rate can be charged;

  (In any case, the question – whether the self-employed should pay only the *employee's* part of the contribution or the *total* rate, including the employer's part – needs to be addressed).

- where social security contributions are determined by or tied to the income tax authority's (annual or half-yearly) assessment the health insurance contribution might also be so tied;

- the self-employed may pay a flat-rate or a minimum contribution;.

- the income assessment of self-employed might be made on the basis of property (land, workshops, shops, inventory, houses or other objects) which may indicate the ability to pay;

- for the self-employed, membership may be voluntary (e.g. until a certain age, after which they will have no access to social health insurance);

- a different benefit package can be made available for the self-employed (e.g. for catastrophic risks only);

- the self-employed may get only cash benefits which are directly linked to the level of contributions paid. For this cash they can "buy" health services.

Casual workers Casual workers represent another group which is difficult to embrace in a health insurance scheme. By its very nature, casual employment is difficult to define and control, registration is administratively difficult and contribution collection systems are also very difficult to operate and monitor.

Rural majority Developing countries often face additional problems for many have a small industrial sector and a large rural sector. Industrial and city populations in some countries constitute as little as 20% of the total population with rural communities accounting for as much as 80%. Coverage of such a large rural majority raises major technical and administrative problems for a health insurance scheme, not least in the assessment and collection of contributions (as explained previously).

D. Administrative implications

A social health insurance scheme involves a range of administrative functions including:

- the identification and registration of insured persons;
- the collection of contributions;
- establishing and monitoring arrangements with providers;
- processing claims;
- making payment to providers;
- maintaining records of claims and entitlements;
- accounting and collecting statistics;
- financial management.

The scale of these tasks depends on the size of the proposed insured population but constraints relating to the infrastructure in the country and to the level of education will also be reflected in the effectiveness of the administration. As pointed out in previous paragraphs, inclusion in the scheme of particular groups often introduces major administrative challenges – if not problems.

An assessment should therefore be made, at a very early stage, as to whether there is the capacity to efficiently administer a social health insurance scheme, whether this will entail establishing a new institutional structure or whether it will be feasible to make use of existing administrative systems, such as a social security pensions scheme or a system for the collection of income tax.

There are strong similarities between the administration of a social *health* insurance scheme and a social insurance (social security) scheme. The second manual in this series – *Administration of Social Security*[3] – deals with many aspects of administration which are equally relevant to health insurance schemes (coverage and registration, collection and recording of contributions, compliance and enforcement, benefit procedures, public relations, institutional management, etc.).

E. The health care infrastructure

Clearly, a demand for health care, generated through the introduction of a compulsory social health insurance scheme, must be matched by supply and distribution of services. Health insurance gives the insured population an entitlement to health services and the successful development of social health insurance depends, in part, on the availability of high quality and appropriate health services for the insured population. It is clearly essential that the infrastructure exists to provide those services which, in turn, will add to the incentives to comply with the requirement to pay toward the scheme.

It is also important that scheme members *do* have better access to health care *if* they pay contributions. These contributions are a payment mechanism for title to care when it is needed. This entitlement obviously has to be matched by a commitment by the scheme, otherwise the members will be reluctant to continue paying contributions.

However, when social health insurance is introduced, it is often difficult to offer immediate and visible advantages to members by way of better access to care. Most countries have a system of access to some form of *emergency* care, regardless of the individual's ability to pay – or of their insurance status.

The introduction of user fees in public hospitals and health centres may not be slow and lax. The bottom line is .... people will rightly question the advantages of the health insurance scheme unless it brings additional – and demonstrable – benefits, or when increasingly high user fees are rigorously charged.

The existing provision of health care services will often reflect past developments – revealing a mixture of private, charitable, religious and government initiatives. Reforms may also have

---

[3] ***Administration of Social Security*** – (Manual No. 2 in this series) Social Security Department, Geneva, 1998 ISBN 92-2-110735-3

taken place, for example, to modify health service patterns of delivery, to increase the comprehensiveness of the system, etc. The result of such developments, however, is often a health care system which has marked variations and disparities between regions and between rural and urban areas. Other legacies may include a focus on hospital services but little or no primary care and a very low status of those health care professionals who work in rural areas. Even where necessary skills are identified as being needed, they are often lacking. Over time, a decrease in public expenditure at national and regional levels may lead to considerable under-funding of public health services.

Under schemes which preceded the introduction of the health insurance scheme, supply problems may have related to the absence of facilities, or of medical staff, or of drugs, or from shortages, or a lack of quality. The social health insurance scheme *must* be seen to be making a difference to this situation – and a difference which is sufficient to justify the contribution imposed. This may be particularly difficult where the existing system is funded by the State and is free or heavily subsidised for the patient, and where immediate resources are not available to improve the quality of services. Different approaches may be adopted to this problem, for example by:

- guaranteeing easy access for insured persons;
- establishing special units, within public hospitals and clinics, where the quality of service is higher;
- channelling resources from the social insurance fund back to those units which have provided the care;
- introducing user fees for health care either in advance of, or at the same time as, the health insurance scheme (user fees would not be paid by insured persons and their families).

Three fundamental questions must also be addressed at an early stage in the planning process:

- whether the scheme will be able to provide significant advantages, in terms of benefits to those insured under it, without disadvantage to other sections of the population;
- whether the infrastructure exists to provide the health care entitlement which is envisaged under the scheme everywhere in the country – where there are insured members;
- whether there is a chance to improve deficient health services within a reasonable period of time – for example through collaboration between the Ministry of Health and the health insurance scheme?

Unit 3: Issues for planning

It is crucial to recognize, throughout the planning and implementation of a health insurance scheme, that individual countries will have quite specific issues which need to be addressed. Even when the issues are similar, the consequences of their interaction will vary considerably. An example of this is the different responsibilities held by different government ministries, from one country to another, and the impact that this has on access to information, span of consultation, and influence within the Government.

There are a number of major subject areas to be addressed once a decision has been made to plan or revise a social health insurance scheme. These include:

- assessing the current situation;
- defining the key elements, in terms of population coverage and health care benefits;
- estimating expenditures and revenues;
- determining the institutional structure;
- elaboration of a draft law;
- determining the process of change.

Most of these areas will be re-visited in later sections of the manual.

The following table provides an overview of these issues and the questions to be raised in their context.

Steps	Questions (examples)	Who will do it?
Assessing the current situation	1. What is the need of the population? 2. How does the labour market look like? 3. What is the level of income? 4. How does the health infrastructure look like? 5. What are the interests and probable positions of the concerned groups?	Specialized institutes, planning departments of ministries
Defining the key elements	1. Coverage 2. Benefits	Government
Estimating expenditure and revenues	1. What will be the cost of the planned benefit package? 2. What will be the necessary contribution?	Specialized institutes, planning departments of ministries
Determining the institutional structure	1. How will the administration look like? 2. Who will be the providers? 3. How will they be accredited and paid?	Specialized institutes, responsible ministries
Elaboration of a draft law	1. How to device the planned scheme so that it fits into the legal and institutional structure of the country? 2. How to elaborate the practical details of the planned scheme so that the regulations will be applied?	Responsible ministries, government, specialized institutions
Determining the process of change	What will be the next steps to be taken?	Planning departments of ministries, specialist institutions

SOCIAL HEALTH INSURANCE

MODULE 2:
DESIGNING A SOCIAL HEALTH INSURANCE SCHEME

International Labour Office   International Social Security Association

SOCIAL HEALTH INSURANCE

MODULE CONTENTS

Unit 1 **Coverage**

    A. Who will benefit from social health insurance?

    B. Voluntary membership

    C. Planning issues

Unit 2 **The health care benefits**

    A. What type, quality, and costs of health care are people accustomed to?

    B. How can this situation be improved by health insurance?

    C. What will the benefit package cost?

MODULE 2

DESIGNING A SOCIAL HEALTH INSURANCE SCHEME

Introduction

This module addresses the two basic elements of a health insurance scheme:

- Coverage of the population

and

- The benefits to be provided.

It analyses the options and elaborates the key questions for the planning process.

Unit 1: Coverage

A. Who will benefit from social health insurance?

ILO Conventions provide some minimum standards of population coverage which, even for those countries which have not ratified the Conventions, represent guidelines for policy decisions and gradual development. The Conventions require that health care will be provided to employed persons but that, in *all* cases, coverage should include the dependants of the insured workers – that is, spouse and dependent children.

Ideally, the social health insurance scheme should cover the *whole* population, both to provide the protection derived from insurability and to extend the scope of solidarity on which the scheme is based. As explained previously, however, there are invariably obstacles and arguments against seeking universal coverage in the first stage and that these are based on political as well as administrative and economic considerations.

Administrative considerations ... ... may include the fact that there might be population groups who are very difficult to register and whose income is difficult to assess B a basic requirement for a functioning health insurance.

Political considerations ... ... may include the fact that there are groups which do not want to be included in a system with broader solidarity – for example because they already benefit from health care provisions.

Economic considerations ... ... especially take account of the inclusion of the non-active sections of the population – dependants, pensioners, and other groups with no primary income.

One of the criticisms levelled at social health insurance is that, rather than improving equality of access to health care, a social health insurance scheme can entrench inequality. Given that it is fairly straightforward to identify and collect contributions from the section of the population employed within the *formal sector*, it is likely that this sector will be the starting point for the social health insurance scheme.

There is a danger, however, that the scheme may never extend *beyond* the formal sector of the workforce and their dependants. This is because of the difficulties (already partly explored in Module 1) of identifying those in the informal, the self-employed, the casual worker, and the rural sectors, and the problems associated with collecting contributions from them and enforcing compliance. Thus, large portions of the population are denied the opportunity of participating in a solidarity-based health insurance scheme.

Ironically the groups who are thus excluded are those least able to contribute, whose need for health care may well be higher – but whose access to good health facilities lower – than those who are able to participate in the scheme from the outset.

There may be resistance to coverage by those who consider themselves to be already adequately protected for health care. Special schemes may already exist, for some groups, for a range of social protection measures – e.g. free medical care for civil servants and members of the armed forces – and government may prefer to maintain such arrangements. However, the exclusion of special groups (such as public servants) can lead to pressure from *other* groups of workers who also have their own employer-based arrangements for medical care and who consider that they too should be excluded from coverage under a national social health insurance scheme. For example, in Thailand, employers who are able to show the social insurance institution that they provide medical care for their workers, which is at least as good as that provided under the national social health insurance scheme, may be exempted. In the long-term and given the mobility in employment, it is not in the interest of the worker to be exempted from the general scheme which will guarantee portability. In Pakistan, for example, all workers who earn above a prescribed amount are excluded from coverage since it is presumed that they are adequately covered by other arrangements.

To some extent however, the pressure for exemption from coverage may simply reflect a reluctance to participate in a risk pooling scheme. Since such a scheme is typically financed by earnings-related contributions it provides the same level of benefit to all. High wage earners, particularly those with few or no dependants, will see themselves as shouldering a disproportionate share of the burden of expenditure under the scheme. If, however, too many concessions are made in the face of such pressure, the risk-pooling basis of the scheme will be prejudiced and the individual cost will then be higher. If a social insurance scheme is to succeed in its objectives, it must cover a *wide* range of risks – not only those who are "bad risks", e.g. pensioners or large families – and it must do so on a compulsory basis. The fund, too, will be compromised if enterprises with higher wage earners are exempted.

Compulsory membership can be justified as "a contract between generations" since, at some point, most people will eventually become a bad risk, in particular when they have families or as they grow old. Therefore single and young people, who pay high contributions, can be seen as investing in their coverage for health care.

It is usual for some limits to be applied to the level of health care provided under the social health insurance scheme. This gives some opportunity for employers or individuals to arrange supplementary provision – but while still participating in the general scheme.

Policy on coverage will also have to take account of administrative feasibility. The pattern may have already been set by an established social security scheme which is already providing other benefits. It is common, in developing countries, for such schemes to temporarily exclude the smaller employers[4] on the grounds of administrative expediency. Small employers being considered the least likely to understand the obligations of the scheme and perhaps who may also be operating on a rather precarious financial basis with tight margins. Additionally, the social security administration may not have the initial capacity to ensure compliance among small employers who are likely to be numerous and, particularly in urban areas, often difficult to identify. In some countries (India, for example) a reverse approach is adopted – employers in prescribed occupations or areas are covered and those who are *not* prescribed are exempt. The ultimate objective, however, is to develop the capacity to cover *all* – even the small enterprises.

In many countries, the intention is that coverage will gradually be extended as the economy and capacity of the social security administration develops but, in practice, there are often long delays in that process, particularly where legislation must be enacted. (It is interesting to note that, of the 172 countries included in *Social Security Programmes Throughout the World*[5], only 54% are shown to have health care coverage provided in addition to cash sickness and maternity benefits).

The administration of a social health insurance scheme has an additional dimension which needs to be taken into account when considering the feasibility of establishing broad coverage. Since entitlement to health care *should* (as stated in ILO Convention 102) include family members, it is desirable for all dependants to be registered. It is very difficult, however, to produce (and especially to maintain) accurate and up-to-date registration of persons who are indeed the legal dependants. The definition of family members may be rather loose in some societies with an extended family living in the

---

4   The definition of "small employer" varies from country to country but, typically, refers to an employer with fewer than five or ten or – more rarely – one hundred employees.

5   *Social Security Programmes Throughout the World.* Social Security Administration, Office of Research and Statistics. (SSA Publication No.13-11805, July 1997) ISBN 0-16-048224-0

same household. It is also very difficult to detect fraudulent claims which are made in respect of fictitious family members.

A social health insurance scheme, originally established for formal sector workers, may be difficult to extend to the self-employed or to those without an identifiable employer because in such cases there is no obvious source for an "employer's contribution".

In the case of those in receipt of another social security benefit (pensioners, the sick, the disabled, the unemployed, etc.) it may be possible for the social health insurance fund to receive a transfer of resources from the social security fund and for this amount to be taken into account in the funding of that scheme.

For those working on their own account, however, there is no employer and therefore any contribution to a social insurance scheme would have to reflect the *combined* liability of the "employer" and "employee". This problem is not insuperable and has equal application to other social security benefits but it tends to compound the difficulties of identifying such persons, determining their incomes, and ensuring compliance. It is worth noting, for example, that in Turkey – where there is a special scheme for the self-employed, under which insured persons are obliged to pay a contribution which provides entitlement to health care and to pension benefits – the vast majority contribute at the *minimum level* required to satisfy the entitlement conditions.

Especially in those countries where the majority of workers are in the informal sector, there are great practical difficulties associated with identifying and registering contributors, assessing income levels and arranging for contribution collection. Module 1 included a reference to the fact that, in these circumstances, coverage of the whole population – which is usually the expressed intention of those promoting the concept of national social health insurance – is unlikely to be realized. However, there are an increasing number of innovative experiments, some of which have proved successful, in incorporating the informal sector into a social health insurance scheme, or in developing social health insurance schemes which are specifically geared to the needs of the informal sector.

A special challenge is the inclusion of the population in the rural environment. Problems that exist here are:

- the lack of communication infrastructure;
- the large distances and wide distribution of the population which makes it difficult to address and identify them;

- the weak health infrastructure which makes it difficult to provide acceptable health care in return for the contributions paid.

Another issue of coverage is the inclusion of the non-active population. To this group belong

- dependants of the insured active population,
- the pensioners and
- other recipients of social benefits.

The dependants group may be very large in some countries and it may include:

- a spouse

    (and it should be remembered that, in some countries, men may have several spouses and, moreover, in many countries spouses work in the informal sector);

- children – up to a certain age;
- parents (if there is no pension scheme).

If these groups *are* included, their health care costs have to be paid either from the contribution income from the active insured members, from the revenue from other social contributions, or from tax revenue. There is no primary income which could be an assessment base for social health insurance contributions. Thus, the cost of the including these groups is a political issue.

The following table gives an overview of population groups that may be covered by social health insurance.

Population group	Technical feasibility	Political feasibility	Contribution payment
Active population			
1. Formal sector employed	Registration and contribution deduction relatively easy	Some groups do not want to be included	Employer and employee
2. Informal sector employed	Registration and contribution collection difficult	Sometimes the concept of insurance is not understood. Because of very low income people do not want to pay.	Employer and employee
3. Self-employed	Income assessment, registration and contribution collection difficult	The self-employed with higher income often do not want to be included	Self-employed worker (full contribution or only employee part?)
4. Rural workers	Income assessment, registration and contribution collection difficult	Weak health infrastructure, which makes it difficult to provide a certain standard of benefits	Workers and employers
Inactive population			
1. Dependants	Definition of family sometimes difficult	Costs of inclusion is often an issue	No contribution or (in some countries) contributions paid by the State
2. Pensioners	Registration and contribution collection relatively easy	Costs of inclusion is often an issue	Contribution paid by pension fund or (in some countries) by the State.
3. Recipients of social benefits (unemployment benefit, social assistance etc)	Registration and contribution collection relatively easy	Costs of inclusion is often an issue	Contribution paid by the State

B. Voluntary membership

It will have become abundantly clear that it is very difficult to create a system which covers the *whole* population right from the start and some countries therefore use the facility of voluntary membership as a way of achieving wider coverage.

Fig. 6:
"... clear that it is ... difficult to create a system which covers the whole population ..."

If access to the scheme is offered on a voluntary basis the registration of members will result from their own initiative. However, the problems associated with coverage of family members – and with assessing the level of contributions – still remain.

Some groups will be enticed to join the scheme by the offer of voluntary membership, particularly those not presently covered by an insurance scheme and those who are dissatisfied with the existing quality of health care services.

At the same time, however, voluntary membership may result in the scheme attracting too many "bad risk" groups and insufficient "good risk" groups. Voluntary membership may also increase the risk of adverse selection and abuse of the scheme. It is also likely that people will choose not to join the scheme whilst they are healthy but, if they fall seriously ill, will then want to apply for membership.

One way of reducing abuse is to require qualifying contributions, for example:

- allowing pensioners to participate *only* if they have been members for a minimum period (perhaps half of their working life);

- establishing a maximum age for joining the insurance scheme;
- insisting on a qualifying period of, for example, six months – during which new members pay contributions but are not allowed to claim benefits; this is in order to prevent people joining only when they actually fall ill;
- limiting voluntary access, for example by providing only one opportunity to join the scheme (perhaps during the first year of working activity or once in the lifetime).

Voluntary membership is clearly only likely to be taken up where individuals perceive it to be in their own best interest. Even when this perception turns out to be incorrect there is often a tendency for "voluntary members" to ensure that they recover their expenditure – that is they ensure that claims are made in order to "recoup" their contributions.

C. Planning issues

At the early planning stages of a social health insurance scheme it is crucial to project the numbers and location of those who will benefit from the system and this leads to a number of factors which need to be addressed. Answers to the following questions should provide the basis for more clearly identifying the number of people likely to participate in the scheme, the progression of anticipated coverage, and the location of contributors.

- *Will participation in the scheme be voluntary or compulsory?*
- *What is the target population?*

    (Will the social health insurance system cover the whole population or will it initially cover only formal sector employees – or even only a sub-sector of formal sector employees – and will it cover self-employed?).

- *How will it be possible to overcome the technical problems of the registration of and contribution collection from certain groups?*

    (For example informal workers and self-employed).

- *Who will be the main groups that might oppose their inclusion into the health insurance? Are they necessary in order to achieve a reasonable risk mix or a solidarity on the income side? Are there possibilities to convince them?*

- *Is it possible, at an early stage, to identify the number of probable contributors?*

  (Wage earners, self-employed, pensioners etc.).

- *Is it possible to make an estimate of the revenue from contributions?*

  (On the basis of income and number of contributors).

- *Is it possible to identify the average number of dependants?*

  (In Thailand, for example, the average number of dependants is 2.5 per contributor and in the Philippines the figure is 5 per contributor. The difference makes a potentially huge impact on the package of care which can be afforded).

- *Will other exemptions from contributions be permitted – which means that there will be individuals receiving benefits without paying?*

  (If so, who and why?)

- *Is it possible to quantify the number of persons which will be exempted from contributing to the social health insurance scheme but will nevertheless receive benefits?*

- *Can reasonable projections be made about the likely changes in proportion of the population benefiting from the scheme over a ten to twenty year span?*

  (For example, what is the current and projected birth rate in the country?).

- *Do some of the population groups already benefit from an insurance system – e.g. community-based or employment-based groups?*

  (It is often the case that groups of employees, such as military personnel and civil servants, already have health care packages as part of their terms and conditions of employment).

- *If there are existing schemes, will those schemes be incorporated into the new social health insurance scheme or will they continue independently?*

- *If they continue independently, will those participating in these schemes be exempted from the wider social health insurance scheme?*

- *Can reasonable projections be made about the increase in proportion of the population liable to contribute to the scheme, as coverage increases?*

Unit 2: The health care benefits

Introduction

One of the reasons for promoting the concept of a social health insurance scheme in a country is to herald the prospect of improved health services for those contributing to the scheme. It is important that services are planned which *do* reflect a higher standard of care and treatment and which provide easier access than beneficiaries had previously been used to.

The ideal benefit package for a specific country or region will depend on a variety of considerations. Such a package should clearly deliver the kind and level of health care services which are necessary to maintain and promote good health but it is also important, as part of the planning process, to have regard to cost-effectiveness in the delivery of health care services.

In determining what services will be provided under the social health insurance scheme, it is crucial to retain cognisance of the health culture of the country. But, when planning the benefit package, there are many other issues to consider and these are referred to in this Unit.

Basically the following questions need to be answered:

- What type, quality and costs of health care are people accustomed to?

- How could this be improved?

- What would this improvement cost and would it be affordable with the projected income of the insurance?

A. What type, quality and costs of health care are people accustomed to?

A number of issues need to be addressed, questions asked and information obtained but that information will not necessarily always be available in the form of compact statistics. Some of the data and information required *will* be available but in crude form; some will be no more than an educated guess; some will simply be unavailable. However, the information to be sought should include, the following.

- To which kind of health care do people have access?
- Do they have to pay?
- Who are the major care providers in primary, secondary and tertiary care?
- Where are the major care providers located?
- (An attempt should be made to identify a geographical distribution of facilities in each category).
- What kind and quality of care do they provide?
- What are the main deficiencies of the current health care provision?

The Ministry of Health will be an obvious starting point for much of this information, particularly its Department of Planning. Information may not be available in the format needed or be presented in a "straightforward" way; indeed it may sometimes only result from a series of discussions with Ministry of Health officials, perhaps at different levels.

Other potentially useful information sources will include UN organizations who have assisted with planning, development or implementation of health related projects, bilateral donors who have invested in earlier projects, and development banks.

Information on the private health sector may be available directly from these schemes and providers or – where one exists – from a national association of private providers. In most countries, private providers are required at least to register their facilities with the Ministry of Health, even where they are not required to be accredited to provide health care. The Ministry of Health will therefore usually be able to provide a full list of private health operators and their locations.

B. How can this situation be improved by health insurance?

The following questions need to be answered before the package of benefits can be determined.

- What are the priorities for health care under the social health insurance scheme?
- How will primary care be provided and what will be included in the package?
- Will secondary care be provided and, if so, what will be included in the package?

- Will tertiary care be provided and, if so, what will be included in the package?
- What services, in all three levels, will be explicitly *excluded* from the package?
- Can the existing health care infrastructure of the country support the planned benefit package, or will there be a need for additional training of professional staff, or investment in the building and equipping of facilities?

Major diseases in the country

Major causes of death in the country

The top 5-7 causes of death should give a fair idea of where resources should be focused.[6] This information will be readily available if the country is a WHO signatory, for whom therefore it is compulsory to code causes of death using the International Classification of Diseases (ICD) and to submit the information to WHO on an annual basis.

Major reasons for hospital admission

Patients may be admitted for various reasons – illness, maternity, work-related and non-work related accidents. As other financing mechanisms, including social security benefits, may exist for these contingencies, it is important to have these data in the planning stage.

Major causes of hospital discharge

These can be found from the diagnoses assigned to patients on discharge from hospital. Most countries keep some record of this, ranging from detailed coded data showing main diagnoses and co-morbidities of each patient to vague notes in the medical record indicating the main symptom presented. At worst, and in the event that neither of these sources yields the appropriate information, site visits to hospitals and discussions with experienced and knowledgeable clinicians in the major specialties will give a reasonable indicator of hospital morbidity patterns.

Preventative health services provided to the whole population (community health services) also need to be identified. It may well be that these services are entirely adequate in terms of quality, quantity and accessibility, and there will be little point in adding to the financial burden on the social health insurance fund by including the services in the benefits package. The following services are normally provided by government on a national basis:

---

[6] In some countries, however, private hospitals are not required to submit data to the Ministry of Health. This means that the epidemiological picture which is available may be distorted, excluding those who can afford to pay for private health care and whose health status would normally be expected to be higher than those who cannot afford to pay.

- immunisation
- family planning.

It is essential that there is full coordination between the Ministry of Health and the other agencies involved in the provision of health services in order to ensure that the insured population will not be excluded from the services generally available.

New health insurance organizations in any country run a major risk of failure during the implementation and early operational stages. Extensive education of potential beneficiaries needs to be undertaken in order to ensure the successful implementation of a scheme, even where participation in the scheme is compulsory. Contributors understandably want to see evidence that their contributions are actually being spent on the promised much improved health care. Rational utilization behaviour by the members is, in itself, an objective. In countries with a history of mismanagement of funds, this is all the more important.

Often the managers of social health insurance funds are so anxious to show that resources are not being mismanaged that they feel obliged to provide contributors with whatever is considered to be "visible evidence" of the application of the resources. One of the main priorities of social health insurance should be to identify – and arrange provision for – health care which is most appropriate to the beneficiaries. It can be shown that good *primary* health care is the optimal foundation to improve and maintain health status – and it is also cost effective.

Primary health care has the disadvantage of being "undramatic" and therefore may lack appeal in marketing terms. It is difficult to promote because it aims to *reduce* illness and limit disease and this really depends on the disease pattern and culture.

If there is a practice of going directly to hospital for treatment of minor illnesses, or an equally strong tradition of self-diagnosis and self-prescribing, it will be an uphill struggle to educate beneficiaries about the benefits of primary care. Such education *is* essential, however, if the most appropriate care *is* to be given and if controlling costs is to be an important feature of the health insurance scheme. The practice of going directly to hospital may be linked to the lack of primary health care in the community.

It is important that primary care should be the first point of contact with health services. Primary health care, properly established and controlled, with an effective referral mechanism, will reduce the demands on secondary and tertiary care which are significantly more expensive.

Establishing primary care as the *first* point of access to health services will make a major impact in controlling overall costs and workload. Furthermore, establishing a referral requirement from a primary care practitioner to gain access to secondary care (for all but emergencies) will significantly reduce the workload of secondary providers.

Fig. 7:
"It is important that primary care ... be ... first point of contact ... with health services ..."

A further reinforcement of that principle can be made by building disincentives into the system which discourage patients from presenting themselves at the secondary level for anything but emergencies. These disincentives could include, for example, a significant fee being charged to a patient who presents for treatment at secondary level without having a referral from a primary care provider, where the presenting symptoms do not constitute an emergency. Where there is a general lack of doctors in a country, nurses and paramedical health personnel can carry out major primary care functions.

It is often the case that primary care has been so neglected over the years that insufficient numbers of qualified and competent professional staff would be available to provide an appropriate primary care service, if one was established. If primary care is to be the basic benefit of the social health insurance scheme this issue will need to be addressed early in the planning phase. Establishment of a post-graduate primary care practitioner programme can be arranged through strong liaison with the medical schools, and the Ministry of Health, and by accessing international assistance. In the absence of in-country training, other countries, where primary care is an established feature of health provision, are often willing to make primary care training available.

The status and remuneration of the primary care doctor also needs to be taken into account. If the doctor is considered to be of a "lower status" than a hospital doctor, then there will continue to be problems of acceptability for primary care as the first point of contact with the health services.

The drugs to be included in the benefit package will also need to be decided. While it is understandable that the health fund will want – and need – to control its resources, it is equally important that the patient has access to both diagnostic services *and* treatment under the scheme. Nevertheless, the cost to the health insurance fund of providing drugs should not be underestimated. Often a compromise is reached by the fund agreeing to make prescribed drugs available free of charge if they are included in an agreed essential and generic drug list. The fund may then exclude the provision of drugs which do not require a doctor's prescription and may be purchased over-the-counter.

It should also be noted that the drug provision requires close contact between *all* the government agencies involved – in relation to purchasing policy, quality control, storage, distribution and pricing policy.

Decisions will have to be taken about precisely what is to be included in the benefits package under the social health insurance scheme. Those decisions will depend on the type and quality of treatment already available in a country, on the priorities for health provision to beneficiaries, and on the anticipated resources accruing from contributions. Rather than provide a list of every eventuality it is often useful to suggest, in the first instance, a possible list of services which would be excluded as benefits. These are usually non-medically necessary services, such as cosmetic surgery. Other exclusions may be care covered by other mechanisms such as motor vehicle accidents, natural disasters or civil strife.

C. What will the benefit package cost?

Basically there are three approaches to estimating the costs of a benefit package -

- the supply oriented approach
- the demand oriented approach
- the combined approach.

The **supply oriented** approach is based on an estimate of the necessary infrastructure (facilities, staff), especially:

- Primary care facilities
- Secondary care facilities
- Tertiary care facilities.

Each of them is taken into account only if they are covered by the health insurance and if they treat exclusively health insurance patients. The costs of this supply is taken as cost for benefits of the insurance. This technique has advantages and disadvantages:

- Advantages -
    - it is relatively easy to calculate and
    - data is normally available.
- Disadvantages -
    - it does not respect possible changes in costs due to the introduction of the health insurance,
    - it does not respect possible co-payments by patients.

However, estimates are possible by increasing the costs by a certain percentage and by estimating the volume of co-payments.

A more sophisticated way of estimating the cost of a benefit package is the **demand oriented** approach, which is based on the utilization of the health care facilities. This approach is especially necessary if

- facilities are used not only by health insurance patients but also by patients financed from other sources (for example public servants, private patients paying out of their own pocket, patients from other kinds of insurances etc);
- there are different types of co-payment which are related to consumption of goods and services;
- it is necessary to know what benefits can be offered to scheme members.

In these cases it is necessary to obtain data on the *expected* rates of utilization of the services.

As with a number of other factors in the development of a social health insurance scheme, the projection of utilization of health care benefits cannot be entirely precise. Additionally, utilization rates may vary over time, depending on

- the benefits that are eventually included in the package,
- changes in the disease pattern and
- the age structure of the insured population.

Some of the analysis has to be based on estimates and some may be based on pilot projects, studies or surveys to determine current utilization patterns for a defined group (for example, an age group) of the population. Other possible sources of information on utilization include experience from existing schemes and experience from other countries which have similar demographic, epidemiological, economic, and cultural patterns. Difficult though such projections may be, they are an essential feature in the planning of a social health insurance scheme. When the available data are considered incomplete and unreliable, the planning could involve the application of target utilization rates.

For a new scheme, it will be necessary to depend almost entirely on utilization data available from other sources, such as the Ministry of Health and private providers, and to undertake special surveys to obtain estimates of utilization. Where the social health insurance scheme is being revised, data about actual utilization within the scheme over the preceding years should already be available through the information system.

Utilization rates may be based on quite crude or quite detailed factors, for example:

- the number of contacts with facilities per capita (outpatient care);
- the number of bed days (inpatient care);
- units of services provided (number of operations, number of consultations) per capita; (these may be more or less detailed according to the availability of data and the appropriateness of the estimate);
- consumption of certain products per capita (drugs according to some diseases, supplies like prostheses);
- frequencies of diagnosis.

The per capita standards might differ according to the age of the patient and the sex and these rates have to be weighted with costs.

The following table gives an overview over the different types of utilization rates and possible procedures to estimate the costs of these.

Description of unit used	Field of application	Method of costing	Difficulty of getting data on costs	Exactness of estimation	Difficulty of getting utilization data
Number of contacts	Outpatient primary and specialist care	Costs per contact: Total costs of facility divided by average number of patients	Easy	Poor	Easy
Number of bed days	Inpatient care	Costs per bed day: Total costs of hospital divided by average number of patients	Easy	Poor	Easy
Number of services consumed	Outpatient primary and specialist care, inpatient care	Costs per service: Partly direct costing, partly overhead calculation	Difficult	Good	Difficult
Number of products consumed	Drugs, supplies	Costs per unit: Prices	Difficult	Good	Difficult
Number of cases occurred	Outpatient specialist care, inpatient care	Costs per case: Partly average direct costs, partly overhead	Very difficult	Very good	Very difficult

Projecting utilization of health care benefits is influenced by a number of factors. These factors, together with a brief description of how they could affect utilization levels, are referred to below.

Utilization rates are strongly influenced by peoples' age and sex – especially if utilization of certain services is *estimated*.

The age/sex breakdown of the covered population can be used as a crude predictor of utilization, based on data available through the Ministry of Health. As a general guide those who are in regular, formal sector employment, and who are relatively young, relatively fit, and relatively healthy, are likely to use *fewer* health care resources than the very young, the very old or the unemployed.

If only contributors (and not their dependants) are entitled to medical benefits, then a crude case-mix can be determined using epidemiological data from the Ministry of Health. The case-mix has a bearing on the cost of the health benefit package and thus on the contribution rate. Those employed in the formal sector are *less* likely, for example, to have a high incidence of chronic disease (which is more prevalent in the elderly) but are *more* likely to have a higher rate of road traffic accidents. Projected utilization rates *must* be taken into account when assessing the contribution rate.

It should be noted that utilization of health care benefits often lower than predicted in the early years of a social health insurance scheme. This can result from a number of factors including for example:

- lack of awareness and poor public relations, in terms of informing contributors of the health benefits available to them;

- providers being chosen by employers, rather than employees (and which are often therefore not easily accessible);

- the insured not identifying themselves as social health insurance patients when presenting for treatment (and therefore not being captured in the social health insurance statistics).

On the other hand, utilization levels may rise and be higher than the contributions and investments will cover. This can happen where a fee-for-service billing system encourages providers to generate demand for services, or where access to secondary care does not require referral from a primary care practitioner.

Utilization rates should be regularly monitored and reviewed once a scheme is in operation. Changes in utilization patterns over time may reflect changing objectives of the social health insurance scheme. If utilization is falling, it may be an indicator of a reduction in the satisfaction with the quality of care being provided to the insured. It is not sufficient to project utilization rates and then simply accept the utilization pattern as it transpires. Utilization information should be a regular and major feature of management information and should be used to identify changing trends in demography and disease patterns, as well as in technological developments. It is also important to look at variations in utilization rates, over time for the same population and across populations for the same period.

In order to estimate the costs, it is not enough to know the utilization rates. It will also be necessary to know the number of insured who are entitled to benefits. There may be two types of insured:

- contributing members
- dependants.

The number of both must be estimated in order to achieve a cost estimate on the basis of utilization rates.

The number of dependants, in particular, is difficult to estimate. A method frequently used is the assessment or the estimate of dependency rates and to multiply these by the number of contributors.

In the planning phase of the health insurance, however, utilization rates are a useful instrument for estimating costs and for calculating the necessary financial means. Which of the methods described is ultimately used depends on:

- the availability of data;
- the share of the market covered by the planned health insurance. (If the users of the facilities in question are exclusively the patients financed by the health insurance, there might be no need to calculate costs on the basis of utilization rates);
- the patterns of services available in the respective country;
- the benefit package provided by the health insurance;
- the relative costs of the services and products provided;

    (for example if the average cost of a unit of drugs necessary to treat a disease is more expensive than the labour needed – doctor, nurse, clinical officer – there is no use in calculating costs of single services, however it can make sense to calculate, for example, the drug costs according to main diseases).

SOCIAL HEALTH INSURANCE

MODULE 3: PROVIDING THE HEALTH CARE BENEFITS

International Labour Office – Geneva   International Social Security Association

MODULE CONTENTS

Unit 1: **Who will be the partners?**

    A. Direct versus indirect provision of care

    B. Different care levels and providers

    C. Primary care

    D. Secondary care providers

    E. Tertiary care providers

Unit 2: **Provider contracts**

    A. Main characteristics of contracting

    B. The contract partners

    C. Types of contract

    D. Contract contents

Unit 3: **Accreditation of providers and Quality Assurance**

    A. Accreditation

    B. The process of accreditation

    C. Quality Assurance

Unit 4: **Choice of provider for the insured**

    A. Provision of community ambulatory care

    B. Provision of specialized and hospital-based care

MODULE 3

PROVIDING THE HEALTH CARE BENEFITS

Unit 1: Who will be the partners?

Introduction

The provision of health care is a common task of several partners -

- the health insurance scheme;
- the health care facilities (doctors, primary care units, dispensaries, polyclinics, hospitals etc.);
- the Ministry of Health.

It must be clearly understood that the Ministry of Health (or the authority responsible) will continue to supervise the health insurance organization and the health care providers. It is appropriate, at this point, to set out the possible responsibilities of Health Ministries, which are:

- setting overall health policy goals;
- creating the policy framework for the operations and activities of the health funds and providers, and
- monitoring their performance;
- monitoring quality of care;
- ensuring mechanisms are in place to fund and provide training and development of staff;
- ensuring that overall health service costs are kept under control.

It is also important that the social health insurance organization actively participates with the Ministry of Health in defining and making use of the utilization reviews of activities and services.

Identifying *who* will provide the health care package will largely depend on

- *what* package of benefits is to be provided;
- whether to concentrate on providers who work for the health insurance scheme or to be open to the whole market of providers (with corresponding effects on costs);
- what importance is attached to quality aspects.

It is important to begin by recognizing that an individual private health care facility will not necessarily want to become a provider to the social health insurance scheme. Neither will all providers who *are* willing or interested in becoming "providers under the scheme" be acceptable (for example because they do not match the quality standards or are too expensive). Issues such as location of facilities and the accreditation process are also decisive factors. It is often the case that established providers in a country, either providing care under the public health system or being paid directly by patients and private insurance companies under a private system, are reasonably content with the health system as it is, particularly if they can impose user charges without controls. They will often be wary of the concept of a social health insurance scheme. This factor needs to be taken into account and perhaps a programme will need to be undertaken to "sell the concept" of social health insurance to both public and private providers.

A. *Direct versus indirect provision of care*

It is the responsibility of the social health insurance scheme managers to ensure that those who are insured under the scheme have access to the services identified in the health care package. In order to comply with this responsibility, two basic options are available:

(i) Direct provision -

either the social health insurance organization *provides care directly* to beneficiaries through their own clinics, health centres, and hospitals

or

(ii) Indirect provision –

    the social health insurance organization *ensures provision of care* by contracting with health professionals and facilities to provide the care.

In some countries (for example India, Morocco, Turkey and a number of Latin American countries) it is the fund which provides health care directly for its beneficiaries through its own facilities. There are, however, examples of under-used social health insurance facilities standing side by side with over-used Ministry of Health hospitals which do not have sufficient resources to operate them.

While direct provision of care may be unnecessary, it is understandable that, in theory, directly providing benefits allows complete financial and managerial control over the providers. However, the only circumstances where such a decision may be necessary is where professionals or facilities are simply not available within an accessible distance for the insured population. Even in these circumstances it is possible – and in many ways preferable – to encourage providers (either public or private) to *operate* facilities and for the social health insurance organization to contract with them to provide health benefits to those entitled under the scheme. The providers would also be in a position to offer health care to the wider population but would be "guaranteed" an income through participation in the social health insurance scheme. This is a good example of the way in which social health insurance acts as a catalyst to provide improved health care which is more accessible for the *wider* population – not only for those who are insured under the health insurance scheme.

Providing health care benefits directly also implies the building, maintenance, refurbishing, equipping and commissioning of facilities from which to provide the services. The building and maintenance of facilities is an operation which necessitates the employment of a variety of property development and management professionals. For some countries this function becomes a major feature of the social health insurance system; in Turkey for example, the General Directorate of Real Estate and Construction is one of the five directorates of the social security organization (Soysal Sigortalar Kurumu – SSK) with a staff of several hundred.

If a decision is taken to provide health services *directly* to the insured population this will also necessitate the recruitment and training of health care staff, both professional and administrative. In countries where medical and nursing staff are in short supply, recruiting staff specifically for the social health insurance facilities (usually at higher salaries than in the public sector) will serve to exacerbate even further the shortages in other facilities in the country. In some countries, the social health insurance organization will be involved in the training of health workers to assure a balanced supply of the appropriate categories, and assume responsibility for distribution in order to meet members' needs.

The following table gives an overview of advantages and disadvantages of *direct* and *indirect* provision of health care services.

	Advantage	**Disadvantage**
Direct provision through health insurance owned facilities	• Direct control over prices and quality • Planning of infrastructure easier for health insurance	• Bureaucracy • Lack of incentives to provide good quality • Quasi-monopoly • Possible conflicts of interest
Indirect provision through contracted facilities	• Separation of interests • It is easier to cancel co-operation • Better quality due to motivation and competition • Additional sources of income of facilities may also improve quality for health insurance patients • Multitude of approaches in management, ownership, quality and organization. • More flexible	• Qualified managers in the health insurance needed who negotiate • Danger of "under the table" charges and corruption • More legal provisions and frameworks needed.

Before a decision is taken to provide medical services directly under the social health insurance scheme or indirectly by contracts, it is necessary to assess the following:

- the facilities which are currently available, under public and private arrangements;
- the quality and prices of those facilities;
- whether or not there is a geographical disparity
  (whether some areas are better provided for than others);
- which legal pre-requisites are to be fulfilled;

- whether private providers have an incentive and are willing to make contracts with health insurance.

If the facilities which are needed to provide the health care package to the insured population are not available, or are inappropriate or badly commissioned, then the social health insurance fund needs to look at the potential for investing in refurbishing, commissioning or building facilities. If the necessary resources are available, it is also sometimes possible for the health insurance organization and the Ministry of Health to give incentives to private providers to provide or improve facilities. The extra investment brought into a geographical area, through contributions to the social health insurance scheme, may make the refurbishing, commissioning or building of a facility a viable option where previously it was not – especially if it is done in collaboration with the Ministry of Health. This type of investment can take place without the social health insurance fund necessarily having responsibility for the recruitment and training of staff to provide health services or, for that matter, for the upkeep and maintenance of the building.

Establishment of a social health insurance scheme should not be viewed as a mechanism to provide increased resources into an under-funded public health service. It is a welcome and essential by-product of social health insurance schemes that they often afford an opportunity to raise standards of care generally but this cannot be used to transfer the major responsibility for health system development. Establishment of a social health insurance scheme does not absolve the Government of a country from providing basic health care to the total population. What it does allow is that the Government's limited resources can be focused more directly on providing better public health services and care to those who are not yet covered by the scheme.

It should also be noted that the different methods of paying providers each have an effect on the quality of health care services, cost containment, and administration.

B. Different care levels and providers

Normally a distinction is made between three different levels of care:

- Primary care
- Secondary care
- Tertiary care.

At each of these levels there may be different types of providers, which offer the services which are characteristic for each of the levels referred to and the following table provides an overview of the types of providers which may be found.

Level of care	Characterization	Providers
Primary care	• Preventive services • Consultation and basic medical care including dental care, pediatry, gynaecology • Referral ("gate keeper")	• Private GPs and family doctors • Dispensaries and ambulatories • Country hospitals
Secondary care	• Specialized outpatient care • Normal inpatient care	• Private specialists • Polyclinics • Hospitals
Tertiary care	• Highly specialized outpatient care • Specialized inpatient care	• Central hospitals • University hospitals • Specialized private clinics

C. Primary care

Such care is defined by the World Health Organization (WHO) as

"... health care based on practical, scientifically sound and socially acceptable methods and technology, made universally accessible to individuals and families in the community, through their full participation and at a cost that the community and country can afford to maintain at every stage of their development in the spirit of self-reliance and self-determination. It forms an integral part both of the country's health system, of which it is the central function and the main focus, and of the overall social and economic development of the community."

In many countries around the world it has become a common understanding that an efficient primary care network is the best approach in order to achieve

- implementation of preventive objectives;
- a more effective use of scarce resources, especially lower expenses on specialist care and hospital levels;

- accessibility to (at least) basic care for the whole population at bearable costs.

For primary care it is obviously desirable to have a supply of well trained and well qualified doctors, clinical officers, nurses and paramedical health workers located evenly around the country, providing the full range of primary care services. Unfortunately for many countries this is no more than a pipe dream which will be impossible to realize for some years to come.

Before establishing a social health insurance based primary care service, it is essential for the fund to have a clear specification of what constitutes primary care and to identify which services are to be provided to beneficiaries. It is also important to be clear about the payment mechanism for the doctors who will undertake this work on behalf of the beneficiaries. It is argued that the most cost effective payment mechanism for primary care is "capitation" (referred to in Module 5).

D. Secondary care providers

In many countries, hospitals are not only the providers of inpatient care but also of outpatient specialist care. The hospital network should be large enough to give access to these services to all who are covered by the health insurance scheme.

Problems might occur where the density of health insurance patients is very low in some regions of a country, especially in rural areas. This might lead to the effect that certain population groups are, in practice, excluded from specialist and hospital care.

Hospitals tend to reflect the relative wealth of a country and also often reflect the disparity of income between wealthy and poor. Some countries have examples of poorly equipped and poorly staffed public hospitals juxtaposed with very "high-tech" modern hospitals; the former for those who are dependent on public health services and the latter for those who are insured privately (whether individually or through an employers scheme) or who can afford to pay for services out of their own pocket.

Discussions to assess the feasibility or possibility of such development should be held with the Ministry of Health and/or private health organizations. Sometimes the establishment of a social health insurance scheme and the projections for coverage are sufficient to mobilize a health provider into action.

E. Tertiary care providers

Tertiary care is highly specialized care and is provided only through centralized units which tend to be concentrated only in national or provincial capitals.

There has been frequent discussion about the allocation policy in developing countries where, although substantial public resources are often spent on central tertiary care units for the better-off members of society, the poor do not even have the benefit of basic health care services. In some developing countries those who can afford to do so will go abroad to obtain tertiary care treatment. In industrialized countries, tertiary care is normally a part of the health care package offered through social health insurance or the public health service. Few developing countries, however, are able to afford tertiary care services for the larger part of the population.

Fig. 8:
"... distinction is made between three different evels of care ..."

Unit 2: Provider contracts

Introduction

As mentioned before, under social insurance, there are two basic forms of health care provision – the direct and indirect methods. With *direct*, the health fund owns the providers; with the *indirect*, the health fund enters into contracts with providers.

Experience shows that the *direct* method often leads to problems of excessive administration and that the *indirect* method leads to problems of cost control. Most social health insurance schemes use the direct method but there is an increasing interest in the indirect method, particularly as more sophisticated cost control strategies are being developed.

A. Main characteristics of contracting

Contracting between social health insurance and providers may be characterized as follows:

- it is a procedure which regulates the conditions for provision of health care services to those insured under the social health insurance scheme;

- it is one of the main instruments for defining the benefit package;

    (normally the health insurance legislation regulates only the general outline of the benefit package but the details are mostly left to the negotiating partners to regulate – e.g. which kind of services in detail should be provided by a GP, which drug specialities are paid and which are not, which kind of surgery is paid and which is not, etc.);

- the social health insurance organization acts as representative of the insured and thus provides them with an element of consumer protection – especially with price regulation, and the type and quality of services provided.

Contracting is a subsidiary way of regulating health care provision because the state delegates the organization and regulation of health care provision to the health insurance scheme and the independent providers.

B. The contract partners

There are several partners which co-operate within the contracting procedures:

The health insurance organization

This may be the national administrative body which sends representatives to all regions of the country in order to negotiate with providers, it may be regional or municipal branches of the health insurance organization which negotiates, for example, on the basis of framework contracts.

The provider

This may be individual providers – like doctors, clinics or hospitals – which negotiate contracts with the health insurance organization; it may also be associations of providers or chambers which negotiate as representatives of the member institutions. Important in this case is that the federation or association of providers has mandate sufficient to bind their members to the results of the negotiations with the health insurance organization. Providers may be hospitals, GPs and primary care institutions, specialized care providers, dental care providers, producers and traders of drugs and supplies, spas, ambulances etc.

Ministry of Health and supervising agencies

MoH normally sets the legal framework for contracts. This may go into very great detail – including the regulation of the way providers are paid – or it may regulate only the broad framework for the negotiations between the partners. It often also regulates what happens in cases where the partners cannot agree on the conditions of health care provision. In this case, in many countries, it is the MoH which has the possibility to regulate the conditions rather than the negotiating partners.

C. Types of contract

There are several types of contractual agreements which are possible:

Framework contracts

These contracts are elaborated infrequently. They define the general terms of provision – e.g. the benefits covered, the fee schedules, the procedures of calculating payments, quality standards, etc.

Regular contracts

These are generally elaborated more frequently, for example yearly. They assess especially payment levels and tariffs. But they may also contain amendments to the framework contract, for example updates of the definition of benefits.

Other agreements

In addition to the two previous types of contract, which are binding for all partners, there may be agreements of a kind which are less binding and have more the character of recommendations. They provide guidelines for the health care providers for their daily practice. Normally the medical providers, especially doctors, are given a large degree of freedom in order to decide the measures to be taken. They are often only limited by the definition of benefits which are paid, and even then it can happen that doctors will convince patients to pay extra for additional services.

A new approach has been developed which is called *Evidence Based Medicine* (EBM). This approach is based on statistical evidence of the usefulness and the effectiveness of treatments. These experiences are used to provide guidelines to health providers and even for monitoring.

D. Contract contents

There are many elements which can be regulated by contract between the health insurance organization and providers but many of these can also be regulated by the Government or by the MoH. Which elements are regulated by law and which by contract differs from country to country but all of the following elements must be regulated somehow:

- accreditation and admission;
- regulations in case of over- or under-supply of health care facilities;
- the type and quality standards of benefits;
- payment of providers (i.e. the method and form of payment, the level, determination of payment, and payment procedures);
- data exchange and statistics (types of data, recording mechanisms, format of data, data carrier, frequency of data provision);
- utilization of forms and procedures;
- identity and membership checks of the insured;
- Quality Assurance (data basis for monitoring, but also other elements such as opening hours);
- contract duration;
- arbitration procedures.

Unit 3: Accreditation of providers and Quality Assurance

A. Accreditation

It is one of the main responsibilities of the social health insurance fund to ensure that health care *is* available to the insured population. While not necessarily providing that care directly, it is important that the fund has control of the quality, level and types of services provided. To ensure this, the health insurance fund has to set the standards of service, clinical care and facilities to be made available to insured persons. These standards are then used as the basis for accrediting providers; further refinement of the standards are adopted as part of a continuing quality assurance programme.

Recognizing the possibility of disparities in services between urban and rural areas, it is critical to ensure that the accreditation process, established within the social health insurance scheme, reflects the practical realities of prevailing circumstances as well as a commitment to providing improved health care services to the insured.

The accreditation function should be linked to and dependent on the licensing function of the Ministry of Health which has first to set the criteria.

An accreditation process should be established during the planning phase – and certainly prior to choosing providers or implementing the scheme.

What is accreditation?

It is a tool for ensuring that the individuals and facilities, which are accepted by the social health insurance scheme to provide care to the insured population, meet a set of specified criteria. The criteria for accreditation should reflect the minimum standards acceptable to the social health insurance scheme for inclusion on a list of providers. This list could, for example, then be available to the scheme's members, from which they could choose their own provider.

This is so even where the Ministry of Health contracts with the social health insurance scheme to provide a range of services to the insured through public facilities: a "block" accreditation is not to be recommended. Each individual unit, which proposes to provide care, must be accredited or, if they do not meet the standards, put on hold until improvements are made and the facility can be reassessed.

Accreditation by the social health insurance scheme provides a guarantee to the insured population that the providers available to them *do* meet a set of specific criteria. However, it is often the case in developing countries that some individuals and facilities will have vastly superior services to those required by the social health insurance accreditation process. This will more often be the case where providers are available from among both the public and private sectors.

Accreditation does *not* provide any guarantee of a specific workload or income from the social health insurance scheme to the accredited individual or facility. It will be up to the individual providers and facilities to make the services which they offer of sufficiently high quality to attract and retain their share of the insured population.

The accreditation process should be carried out *before* beneficiaries are entitled to access services. Failure to do so would create further difficulties when a provider, who has been permitted to offer services to beneficiaries, subsequently fails to meet the minimum standards established in the accreditation process. No provider, whether at primary, secondary or tertiary level, should be permitted to provide services to beneficiaries unless and until those providers have satisfied the social health insurance fund that the minimum standards *are* being met.

It is self-evident that the accreditation also implies the acceptance of agreed payment mechanisms and of a commitment not to accept any kind of "under the table" payment. Moreover, it is very useful, if the accreditation also implies the use of standard accounting and reporting procedures and formats.

The following table provides an overview of the objectives of accreditation and the effects to be avoided.

Objectives	To be avoided
• To achieve access to health care for the insured • To provide consumer protection for the insured • To achieve a minimum quality • To avoid oversupply • To control costs	• Accreditation is no guarantee for a minimum turnover • To create a process which is so complicated that good quality providers are not interested in applying

B. The process of accreditation

The *accreditation process* should ideally be carried out by staff of the social health insurance fund, trained to elicit information from and review standards in a would-be provider facility. It is not sufficient simply to send out a questionnaire for applicant providers to complete or for a decision to be made on the basis of such a questionnaire. Accreditation *must* be undertaken by health insurance fund staff who are qualified to make judgements and who understand the importance of establishing and maintaining basic standards on behalf of the insured.

The elements to be assessed in an accreditation process are different for primary care than for secondary and tertiary care. They will also have different parameters from one country to another, depending on the prevailing health provision, availability of qualified staff, and of facilities. The following, however, are the basic elements of an assessment:

Community ambulatory care

- Medical qualifications of the doctor (specify the minimum acceptable qualification and preferred qualifications).
- Availability of suitable staff.
- Availability of consulting room (privacy for examinations, examination table, standards of cleanliness, etc).
- Equipment available (sphygmomanometer, blood sugar analysis, height/weight measures, specula, other basic diagnostic test equipment as appropriate).
- Access to more sophisticated diagnostic test equipment, at a local hospital, polyclinic or laboratory.
- Access to drugs, medicines, vaccines and serums, either directly or by prescription from a pharmacy.
- Access to treatments for minor injuries (steristrips, bandages, cat gut and suture equipment).
- Procedures for testing patient satisfaction.

Hospital care facilities

- Minimum number of beds and spacing of beds in wards.
- Minimum numbers of clinical staff – doctors, nurses, laboratory technicians.
- Required qualifications of clinical staff (specify the minimum acceptable qualification and the preferred qualification).
- Minimum ratio of doctors to nurses.
- Minimum ratio of junior doctors to consultants.

- Minimum ratio of doctors to beds.
- Minimum ratio of nurses to beds.
- Availability of operating theatres.
- Availability of recovery rooms.
- Minimum theatre equipment.
- Access to a list of specialties.
- Minimum radiological services.
- Minimum standards for patient record keeping:
- (specify the data elements and information to be kept).
- Maximum waiting times for outpatient appointments and non-emergency in-patient admissions.
- Procedures for testing patient satisfaction.
- Minimum laboratory services.
- Minimum catering standards.
- Minimum housekeeping standards.

Tertiary care

- The same range of criteria as for secondary care but with higher standards specified for:
    - clinical care;
    - qualifications of clinical staff;
    - diagnostic and therapeutic equipment;
    - procedures for testing patient satisfaction.

The accreditation process also needs to be undertaken for any facility which applies to become a provider *after* the start of the social health insurance scheme. It should also be realized that accreditation is *not* a "one-off" activity. It is possible that, once a facility has managed to meet the minimum criteria and gained approval to provide care under the scheme, nothing is done thereafter to maintain or improve its standards. It is important that contracts with providers stipulate that accreditation is an ongoing process and failure to submit to the accreditation process or to meet the standards established by the social health insurance fund – at *any* time – will result in withdrawal of approval for that facility.

Withdrawal of approval has a number of serious implications for beneficiaries, not least of which is the potential inaccessibility of alternative providers. Before approval (for providing health care to beneficiaries) is withdrawn from providers, by the social health insurance fund, the facility (i.e. the provider) should be given a clearly specified and time-limited opportunity to improve standards and refurbish the facility. Failure to comply with the standards at that point will result in approval being withdrawn once the current contract expires. In the intervening period, the social health insurance fund should strive to identify an alternative facility, or a range of facilities, from which beneficiaries can access services and forewarn those facilities that they can expect to be approached by additional beneficiaries.

The obvious longer-term mechanism to adopt, in order to ensure continuing improvements to standards, is to:

retain the basic criteria for accreditation of new applicants wishing to provide services under the social health insurance scheme and

establish a Quality Assurance Programme, by which to improve standards for those with continuing contracts to provide services.

C. *Quality Assurance*

Moving from an accreditation programme into a Quality Assurance Programme (QAP) implies a major commitment to improving and sustaining services. Whereas an accreditation process guarantees the patient a minimum set of standards, the implementation of a QAP presumes that those minimum standards are well met and that facilities – such as those listed below – are now in a position to move forward.

Diagnostic and therapeutic	*Nursing care*
Radiology	*Pathology and clinical laboratory services*
Dietetic services	
Emergency services	*Pharmaceutical services*
Ambulatory/Outpatient services	*Rehabilitation services*
	Health and safety measures
Infection control	*Special care units*
Management and administrative services	*Surgical and anaesthetic services*
Clinical practice (including development of treatment protocols)	*Hotel services*
	High procedural standards of hygiene, security and asepsis
Satisfactory referral arrangements	*Facilities for priority treatment for emergencies*

Objectives of quality assurance

The objectives of a QAP are to actively encourage the raising of clinical, managerial and hotel standards. Standards should be determined with assistance from the relevant professional groups and re-assessed on a regular basis – annually is probably sufficient. The standards need to be set so as to encourage improvement but must also be sufficiently realistic to allow them to be met by, at least some, institutions.

A QAP is dynamic: participation by institutions and units will require involvement from *all* the professional groups, and this will usually create a momentum of its own to achieve higher standards. The standards will also change as health priorities change, and as equipment and clinical techniques become more sophisticated and more readily available.

It is unlikely that a country would be in a position to embark upon a QAP at the outset of a social health insurance scheme. It is more likely to form part of a revision and reform of an existing scheme where, for some years, providers have had an opportunity to become accustomed to providing care at a specified standard and where they are being encouraged to improve further upon that standard.

There are three different kinds of quality which can be checked:

- ***structural quality***

   (infrastructure, equipment, staff, hygiene etc.);

- ***process quality***

   (do the diagnostic and curative procedures meet possible standards);

- ***outcome quality***

   (what is achieved? How is the health status of the patients after treatment?).

The basis of quality assurance is the availability of data – there can be no quality assurance without data. Data may be obtained by -

- statistics, which providers who want to be accredited, have to elaborate periodically, and which are part of a functioning management information system;
- visits to facilities and checks based on standard procedures;
- inquiries among staff and patients.

Unit 4: Choice of provider for the insured

Introduction

The growth of choice and diversity in the provision of health services can lead to more *efficient* health care and an improved *quality* of care and the phrase "*choice of provider*" suggests that the contributors to social health insurance schemes will have a *range* of providers from which to chose. This choice *may* enhance the competition among providers and thus the quality of services provided but, unfortunately however, this is not always the case. There are many instances, particularly in rural areas, where availability of any appropriate health care facility cannot be guaranteed. As pointed out previously, there may be a need for the social health insurance institution either to provide for the establishment or refurbishment of some facilities or to work in collaboration with the Ministry of Health (and/or private health care organizations) to ensure that facilities of appropriate quality *are* available for access to health care by members.

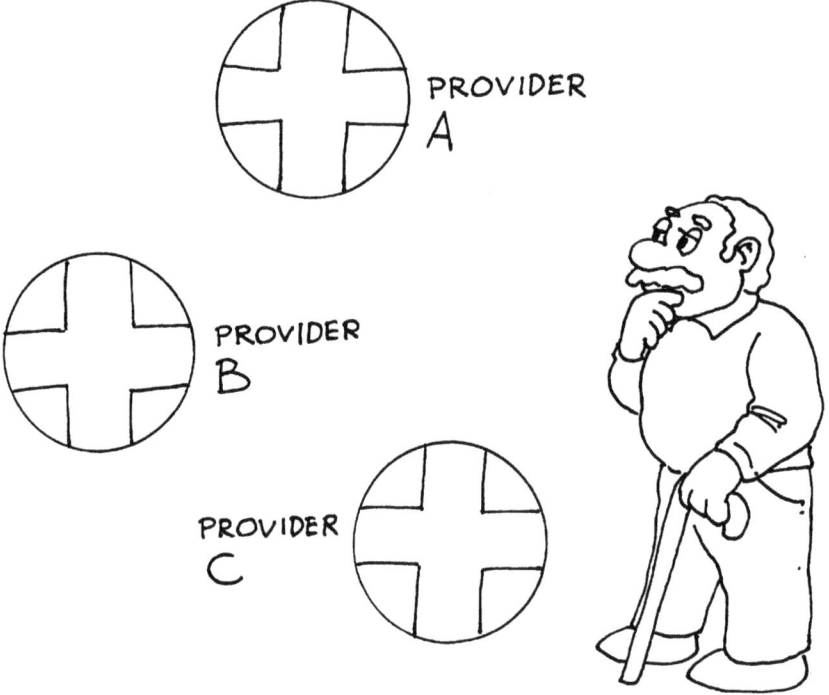

Fig. 9:
"... 'choice of provider' suggests that ... contributions ... have a range ... from which to choose ..."

An example of direct provision is that, in some circumstances, it will even be appropriate for the social health insurance institution to build premises and employ professional and ancillary staff to run them, so that facilities can be available for those entitled to benefit under the scheme.

The situation is rarely this difficult in urban areas, where there is usually an abundance of facilities available which offer health care to contributors. In urban areas a bigger problem is usually one of ensuring that the facilities are prepared to provide the required standard of care to those entitled to benefit under the social health insurance scheme. There may also be a need to limit patient choice in order to give providers the possibility of ensuring continuity and effectiveness of treatment and also to prevent patients from "shopping around". These effects may be achieved, for example, by limiting the possibility to change (e.g. perhaps once – immediately after the first choice – and thereafter only once every 6 months).

A. Provision of community ambulatory care

It has proven useful to introduce some kind of registration mechanisms for providers. This means that patients register with a primary care unit, a pharmacy, or a hospital of their choice. This registration is binding for a certain period and may also be the basis of the payment of the provider.

There are some issues, however, which should be taken into account when designing a registration system and these include the following.

- Where the social health insurance scheme provides coverage for dependants as well as for contributors, perhaps a contributor will prefer to register with a practitioner close to the workplace while the dependants may wish to register with a different practitioner close to their home. Where it is necessary for both the contributor and dependants to register with the same provider, a choice may have to be made between registering with a provider at a location which is more accessible for the contributor or one which is more accessible for their family.

- In order to ensure the advantages of a registration system, a central comparison of registration data is useful in order to prevent individuals from registering with several providers at the same time. This is especially important if the registration is the basis for a later payment of the provider.

- Registration also has to take into account capacities of providers. There should be minimum and maximum numbers of registered patients for each provider.

- Registration implies the need for identification of individuals. This may be relatively easy in small communities but requires certain formalities in urban areas.

All these issues will need to be addressed at an early stage of the scheme's development.

B. Provision of specialized and hospital-based care

It is seen as a problem of registering with secondary care providers that, normally, contacts between the providers and their patients are much less frequent than with primary care units. Many individuals may register only when they have a serious health problem. This is why, in secondary and tertiary provider units, fewer registration systems are applied.

The choice of provider will, to a large extent, depend on the provider payment mechanism adopted by the social health insurance organization. If secondary care is to be paid for through capitation, then insured members will have to register with a *specific* hospital from which they will access *all* secondary care.

This will often, however, pose a problem in the case of treatment for accidents and emergencies which occur when people are away from their registered hospital (for example, when visiting a different part of the country on business, holiday, etc.) for which separate arrangements need to be made by the social health insurance organization.

SOCIAL HEALTH INSURANCE

MODULE 4:
FINANCING
SOCIAL HEALTH INSURANCE

International Labour Office – Geneva   International Social Security Association

MODULE CONTENTS

Unit 1: **Contributions**

    A. Assessing contribution rates

    B. Policy issues and options for assessing contribution rates

    C. Collecting contributions

Unit 2: **Other sources of financing**

    A. Transfers from the State budget

    B. Co-payments

    C. User Fees, Sales, Interest and Fines

MODULE 4

FINANCING SOCIAL HEALTH INSURANCE

Unit 1: Contributions

Introduction

Though social health insurance is mainly financed through contributions, there are other important sources from which it may obtain its resources – the main ones are:

- Contributions
- Transfers from State budget
- User fees and sales
- Others – including fines and interests on reserves.

The issues relating to assessment, collection and recording of contributions, compliance and enforcement, are dealt with comprehensively in another manual in this series – *"Administration of Social Security"*[7]. This unit therefore touches only briefly on these subjects and those who need to know more about contribution issues may therefore wish to refer to that manual (in particular, modules 2, 3 and 4).

---

[7] ADMINISTRATION OF SOCIAL SECURITY – (Manual No. 2 in this series)

A. Assessing contribution rates

There are basically three types of contributions to social health insurance:

- a *flat-rate* contribution

    (which is often used in environments where it is impossible to assess income and wages);

- contribution according to *classes of income*

    (often used for the self-employed);

- contribution as a *percentage of wage and income*.

The first two types may be easier to administer in countries or for population groups where it is difficult to assess wages or incomes accurately.

In many countries contributions are, in some way, wage-related. They may be a percentage of the wage or a fixed amount for people whose wage falls within a certain range.

The *advantage* of wage-related contributions is that they take into account the ability of each individual to pay. Thus everyone can afford social health insurance and this point becomes increasingly important as income differentials in a country rise.

The *disadvantage* of wage-related contributions is that there can be large differences in the level of contributions paid by different individuals for the same benefits. There is a danger that those whose earnings are high will resent paying significantly more than others in the scheme. For that reason, an upper limit (or "ceiling") is often set. Operation of a ceiling means that only the wage or income up to the ceiling is taken into account in calculating the contribution to be paid; no contribution is paid on wages or income above the ceiling.

There is a mathematical formula which can be used for the calculation of a wage-related premium and this is frequently used to determine the overall percentage contribution rate needed to cover the cost of the proposed benefits package, administration, and reserves. This calculation, however, then needs to take into account the feasibility of the rate being acceptable.

The contribution rate % (CR) equals the total annual benefit expenditures plus the total annual administration cost plus necessary annual amount for contingency reserves multiplied by 100 and divided by the total annual amount of insurable earnings – as shown below.

$$CR = \frac{(\text{cost of benefits} + \text{admin costs} + \text{changes in reserves}) \times 100}{\text{total sum of salary}}$$

When assessing contribution rates, one factor to be remembered is that, while the contribution rate is almost always *salary related*, the health care benefit is a *flat-rate* package. Some contributors will thus pay more than others and yet not be entitled to receive any *added* benefits. Similarly, those paying less than others will not be *denied* any benefits. The health care package is an entitlement of *all* contributors – irrespective of the level of their contribution in real terms. In a wage/salary-based contribution system, therefore, the principle of solidarity is clearly in practice.

B. *Policy issues and options for assessing contribution rates*

The package of benefits which it is proposed to make available to insured members will obviously have a major impact on how much it will cost to provide that package. The better and more comprehensive the benefit package is to be, the higher will be the rate of contributions required to meet the cost. The contribution rate must therefore be decided in close collaboration with those determining the benefit package and a compromise needs to be maintained between what is desirable and what is feasible in relation to that package.

While ILO Convention 130 (the 1969 Convention concerning Medical Care and Sickness Benefits) requires social health insurance schemes to provide cover for spouses and dependant children, there are many instances where this has not been done, at least at the outset of a scheme. Where the number of contributors exactly matches the number who are entitled to benefits it is reasonably straightforward to factor this into the calculation of contribution rates.

In many countries contributions are shared, in one way or another, between employees and employers. This may be half-and-half (as in Germany) or the employer may pay the major share of the contribution (as in Spain and Russia).

Fig. 10:
"In many countries contributions are shared ... between employees and employers ..."

It is important that the contribution rate which is set will be sustainable for both employer and employee. Even where the employer contribution rate is accepted as a salary cost, the rate (where it is salary linked) may be sufficient to keep salary levels arbitrarily deflated. Equally, the contribution rate may be a disincentive to employ more staff and thus adversely affect the employment rate. This danger has to be avoided, particularly where the economy is in a development phase.

There is in any case an advantage to having both employer and employees contributing to social health insurance:

- for employees – there is the advantage of feeling the value of the protection which they benefit from and
- for employers – it is important to be a force which is interested in keeping the cost low and thus being a powerful counterpart to provider interests.

The issue often arises of whether the self-employed should pay both employer *and* employee share of the contribution or the employee share only.

- The problem of making self-employed pay both is that this would make the contribution prohibitively high.
- The problem of making them pay only the employee share is that there is then a strong incentive to employ staff on a "self-employment" basis.

Some countries (Romania for example) therefore make the self-employed pay only the employees share of the contribution. Others (e.g. Germany) have the self-employed pay both parts.

Assessment of contribution rates must also take account of whether or not a qualifying contribution period will be required before a contributor (or dependants) is entitled to access the benefits. Some social health insurance schemes insist on ten contributions being made in a calendar year before benefits become available; others require up to 50 contributions to be paid before benefit entitlement begins; yet others allow access to benefits as soon as contributions start to be paid.

There are some obvious dangers in adopting the latter approach in schemes based on voluntary membership, whereby a contributor may choose to make one contribution, access a health care benefit immediately but then make no further contributions until the time when health care is needed again. This practice does not conform to "the sharing of risks or solidarity" and schemes should be so designed as to prevent such abuses.

C. *Collecting contributions*

Given that health insurance schemes are contributory based, it is clearly important to consider the arrangements for collection of health insurance contributions. The administrative arrangements and procedures are, as mentioned in the introduction to this unit, so similar to those for the collection of social insurance contributions – as are also the problems of collection and non-compliance – that the reader may wish to refer to the relevant modules in the *Manual – Administration of Social Security* (number 2 in this series).

However, there is one difference between, on the one hand, schemes administering cash benefits (such as pension schemes and sickness benefit) and, on the other, health insurance schemes. This is that neither the employer nor the employee have an interest in declaring the correct level of income because the benefits are not contribution- related. It is therefore in the interest of both employer *and* employee to declare incomes which are as low as possible. This implies a higher control effort for health insurance in income-based schemes. This is a further reason for having a common income assessment and contribution collection arrangement where there are several contribution-based social security branches.

Unit 2: Other sources of financing

A. Transfers from the State budget

Some countries (for example Slovakia, Russia and Romania) choose to finance part of their social health insurance by State contributions. These transfers are declared to be contributions (and are assessed in the same way as other contributions). The justification is that they are paid for that part of the population covered by social health insurance which has no primary income (e.g. children, housewives, the unemployed, social aid recipients, pensioners).

In other countries, state subsidies to social health insurance are paid for services which are public health related – vaccines, screening, preventative services such as pre-natal care, etc. – but which are paid and organized by the social health insurance scheme.

There are problems in many countries where the State *should* pay a large part of the contributions (as much as 60% in some countries); for example:

- the State often does not fulfil its legal obligations, depending on the current budget situation, which results in deficits for the health insurance scheme and normally the scheme has little chance of getting the state to pay its debts;

- the State, in return for its contribution, demands a large influence on the health insurance scheme which, in effect, makes the scheme a state agency rather than a self-governed body;

- in some countries (Slovakia for example) there were even constitutional problems with the State handing over part of its budget to another agency;

- if all tax payers have access to social health insurance, the only justification for state contributions is from the point of view of equity.

B. Co-payments

Co-payments should be seen as related to social health insurance, even where they are paid directly to the providers and do not, therefore, pass through its budget.

Co-payments are an instrument, defended by advocates who argue that they reduce consumption; this is why they are referred to in French as "tiquet modérateur". Nevertheless, most experts are unanimous that, although they are a useful instrument for gathering funds, for the most part they do not influence patient behaviour. This is because most patients have no influence on the pattern and volume of their consumption – apart from a few exceptions such as dental prosthesis (where prevention can reduce consumption significantly).

There are many different types of co-payments:

- flat-rate co-payments per item or service prescribed;
- co-payments according to the volume (not the price) of prescribed items;
- co-payment according to classes of prices;
- percentage co-payments;
- etc.

In some countries – for example, France – there is a very sophisticated system of exceptions from co-payments for vulnerable and low-income groups and in Germany there is an upper percentage limit of the individual income for all co-payments made in a year.

It should be noted that there are very few health systems around the world which *do not* have a co-payment system. Nevertheless, a distinction needs to be made between "official" and "unofficial" co-payments. In many countries (for example in Africa) although most health care services are free patients who want to obtain health care services often have to pay. One reason is that there is little control over the behaviour of providers and another is that the wages of health workers are very low.

It is therefore very important that the social health insurance scheme has an influence on the co-payments made and is able to ensure that *only* those co-payments which are officially approved are collected from patients.

C. User Fees, Sales, Interest and Fines

Other sources of income for a social health insurance scheme – though not the main ones – are:

- *User fees* and revenues from *sales* of insurance-owned facilities;

- *Interests* on reserves;

  (Health insurance schemes should have reserves equal to 2 or 3 months expenditure in order to be able to ensure proper cash-flow management. The larger the insurance fund, the smaller may be the reserve – because of the arithmetic of risks);

- *Fines*;

  (Health insurance schemes may gather fines for late payments, which are justified by the added cost of collection of the contributions and the lost interest).

SOCIAL HEALTH INSURANCE

MODULE 5: PROVIDER PAYMENT

International Labour Office · International Social Security Association

MODULE CONTENTS

Unit 1: **Provider payment mechanisms**

Fee-for-service

Per case payment

Flat-rate payment

Daily rates

Bonus payments

Capitation

Salary

Budget payment

Special payments

Unit 2: **Issues to consider**

A. Choosing the right payment methods

B. Quality of care and cost containment

C. Administration

D. Which method – and when?

E. Political issues

SOCIAL HEALTH INSURANCE

MODULE 5

PROVIDER PAYMENT

Unit 1: Provider payment mechanisms

Introduction

An earlier unit made reference to the fact that there are many different methods for paying providers and that each method has a different effect on

- the quality of health care services,
- on cost containment,
- and on administration.

Social health insurance schemes consist of

- an insurance body – the health fund and
- those who are insured – the scheme members

but there is also a "third party" – the provider (unlike other social security branches, pension schemes for example) and without providers – hospitals, doctors, nurses, etc. – there can be no health care. Providers represent the "spending side" of social health insurance.

Health care expenditure is determined by two factors – the quantity of services and products that are prescribed or consumed and their price – and both of these are influenced by the system used to pay providers. On the one hand, payment systems must allow providers to achieve a reasonable income – in order to motivate them to produce good quality services, to prevent them moving to better-paid jobs, to prevent them from charging "under the table payments" etc. – but, on the other hand, must also prevent waste and unnecessary provision.

It will therefore be apparent that devising the provider payment system is a very important task, and must balance the quality of care to be made available wich cost containment. The problem of cost containment is an issue in all health services, irrespective of whether the country is developing, in transition or industrialized. Cost containment now commands more attention than almost any other issue in the health care debate. Limited resources and a burgeoning demand for both quantity and quality of health care create a tension which is rarely kept in equilibrium.

Fig. 11:
"Limited resources ... and ... burgeoning demand ... create a tension ... rarely kept in equilibrium ..."

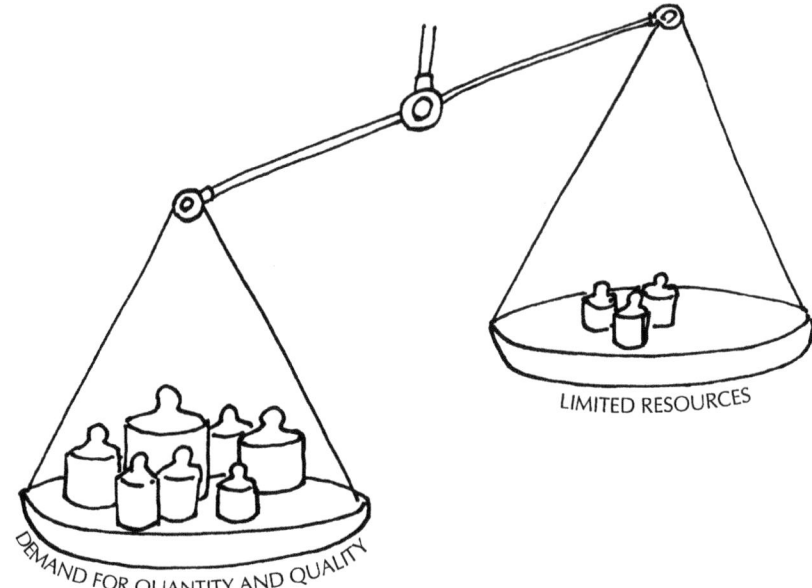

There are a number of well defined provider payment methods, with varying merits and demerits and this unit briefly describes each method. Unit 2 will examine the issues which must be taken into account when decisions are taken on the most appropriate provider payment mechanism.

Fee-for-service

Under the *fee-for-service* arrangement, providers are paid for each item (e.g. each drug of antibiotics) or item of service provided (e.g. an X-ray or medical examination). If the fee-for-service system is *not* controlled, providers will have an incentive

- to charge as much as the market will bear, regardless of whether those who are paying are individuals, private companies, or the social health insurance organization;

- to produce as many units as possible in order to increase the income.

Where the system *is* controlled there is usually an established, regularly revised fee schedule, above which providers may not charge – or beyond which they will not be reimbursed by the third party insurer. Alternatively the providers keep a record of services and items given, on a points basis; the points have a set of values which, when calculated, establish the amount to be paid to the provider.

In some countries, in order to control the number of items produced, there are caps for the total fee volume, which are negotiated for all providers together, per patient, per specialty etc.

Fee-for-service can be used for out-patients *and* in-patients, whether these are individual providers or provider facilities, and also for in-patient or out-patient services. It can be used for all services provided or for certain services only.

Per case payment

Per case payment is often used in combination with diagnosis, but may also be used as flat-rate per case (for specialist care for example).

The costs for treating patients with certain diagnosis are calculated and the provider receives a payment which covers all diagnostic and curative services connected to certain groups of diagnosis. This kind of payment often is used in specialist care and in hospitals. It may also be used in combination with other payment methods. The per case payment best known in the world is the *DRG-payment* (Diagnosis Related Groups) which was developed in the USA and covers about 420 diagnosis.

The problem of the per case payment is the definition of "case".

Flat-rate payment

This method of payment is often used to cover projected costs of equipment, either for an individual practitioner or for a provider facility. An amount is identified by the funding organization together with a detailed specification of what equipment and instruments are expected to be purchased with the payment. Different specifications need to be available for different specialists and facilities. The practitioner/facility is then required to purchase appropriate equipment and then account for the purchase of that equipment.

The flat-rate payment is normally used in tandem with another provider payment mechanism and is often adopted to assist with start-up costs for a new facility or for the replacement of machinery or equipment. It can be used in primary, secondary or tertiary settings, for individual providers or facilities.

Daily rates

Daily rates (also referred to as "per diem fees" or "daily charge") are used mainly for payment to hospitals in respect of in-patients. They are also normally used for the facilities which provide long-term care, since the daily rate is based on a calculation of the total cost of the facility for a year, divided by the number of patient days used. Rates may be increased or reduced in line with cost of living changes during the year for which the payment is due.

Daily rates may be combined with other payment methods – for example with fee for service or with payment per case.

Bonus payments

A bonus payment is paid to physicians or facilities which meet or exceed certain predetermined targets, usually related to the implementation of a national health policy, such as immunization and vaccination rates or screening programmes for preventable diseases. This method is usually supplementary to one of the other payment mechanisms adopted: it is *never* a health systems' *sole* payment mechanism.

A bonus payment is particularly suited to primary care but less so to secondary and tertiary care, though objectives such as a reduction in the overall drugs bill can sometimes warrant a bonus payment at the secondary level. Bonus payments are also used in order to attract providers for remote areas of a country as, in many countries, it is a problem to find providers for rural areas. Bonus payments are sometimes therefore used in order to make these posts more attractive.

Capitation

Capitation – already referred to in earlier units – is a *fee* paid to a provider for the provision of services *for a fixed period*, usually one year, irrespective of what clinical services are required. The capitation fee will either be a flat-rate (per person) or a weighted rate – depending on factors such as age, sex, prevalent chronic diseases and area of residence of the insured.

Capitation is based on the pooling of risk for the provider: the fee takes into account that some beneficiaries may not use the services at all whilst others may use them more often than "average utilization" would indicate. Hence the provider may make a profit on some subscribers and a loss on others. The capitation fee is paid to an individual provider or to a provider facility with whom the insured member is registered. As explained previously, the insured member chooses from a list of approved and accredited providers.

Under the terms of a capitation contract, providers must meet all the necessary clinical requirements of a patient within a given time period. Except in particular circumstances (that is, where a special payment or bonus payment is applicable) the provider has to bear the risk that a patient may use more care than the capitation fee covers. This could lead to a diminution of quality of service or, possibly, denial of access to necessary clinical care. In order to ensure that standards *are* maintained at the appropriate level, the contractual arrangement between providers and the social health insurance fund needs to include an accreditation and quality assurance programme.

The amount of the capitation payment needs to be sufficient to attract the requisite numbers of providers in the country. It must also be a figure which can be met within the financial constraints of the contribution income. In determining the capitation rate, the social insurance organization must be cognisant of Ministry of Health strategies for health services cost containment and balance this against the need to attract appropriate providers.

Capitation is suitable for both primary and secondary care. In some instances a capitation fee is paid to one provider who then has responsibility to ensure *total* health care for the individual – whether primary, secondary or tertiary. As was also pointed out in a previous unit, it is possible to have a "dual capitation" system, with a capitation fee paid to a primary provider and a separate capitation rate being paid to a secondary provider.

The right of the insured to change provider, if not satisfied with standards of service or care, creates an incentive for providers to maintain a *quality* of care. Upper and lower limits are usually imposed on the number of insured people who are registered with each provider. This ensures, firstly, that providers are *not* accepting greater numbers than they have the capacity to deal with (in order to maximise their income) and, secondly, that the age/sex mix and case mix of patients is sufficient to make the resources accruing from the capitation fee economically viable for a provider.

Salary

Under this payment system (used mainly in direct delivery systems) the provider is paid – usually on a monthly basis – for time given, irrespective of the number of patients treated. This type of payment is almost always used where the social health insurance fund owns the facilities from which services are provided and appoints the staff to provide those services. The providers in this case, therefore, reflect the *total* health care team – including medical, nursing, laboratory, ancillary, catering and other staff. A social health insurance fund using salaries as a payment mechanism will also have associated costs to consider. These will include: the recruitment and administration of staff and payment of their salaries; the purchase, maintenance, and amortization of equipment; and the purchase, building or rental, and maintenance of facilities.

The salary payment method is suitable for individuals at primary, secondary and tertiary level. However, where this type of payment system is adopted, salaries are often lower than they would be from an independent provider. In countries where this type of payment system is used, there appear to be few incentives for staff to perform well. (The Turkish social security health insurance scheme is an example, as is the state health care system in Russia). There is also the danger that, if salaries are not competitive, then providers – particularly clinicians and sometimes nurses – will establish an informal fee-for-service system ("under-the-table payments") which effectively denies an access to care for anyone who cannot afford to pay.

Budget payment

This is a payment which is intended to cover the total cost of services provided during a given period, usually of one year. In this case the "cost" includes diagnostic tests, treatments, drugs and medicines. The budget is usually based on historical information about costs, and on negotiations between providers and purchasers of care (usually the insurance organizations).

The historical costs are determined from either

- the actual cost of a unit or from average costs of units of similar size (number of beds, for example),
- the level (secondary or tertiary) and
- the clinical specialty.

For cost-containment purposes, the budget system should theoretically slow the rate of cost increases – which are prevalent with other payment systems. The budget agreed by the purchaser and provider is intended to be a balance between known costs of the unit (such as salaries and overheads) and expected outputs, in terms of numbers of patients treated and their case mix. (A smaller number of patients with complicated aetiology will cost the provider more than a larger number of very straightforward cases).

In the budget payment system, the provider has an incentive to contain costs as much as possible in order to live within the allocated budget. This could result, however, in a reduction in the quality of care and indeed, in some situations, suspensions of hospital admissions where the agreed budget is exhausted. In such a situation the tendency will be to somehow "find additional funds from somewhere" and the net effect is simply to increase the budget.

It is essential, therefore, where this payment mechanism is adopted, to have a formal accreditation and Quality Assurance Programme as part of the contract between the social health insurance organization and providers.

Special payments

Special payments are supplementary to the usual provider payment mechanism, and are made by the social health insurance organization to the provider to cover the costs of particularly expensive treatments which could not be expected to be borne by the provider. This type of payment usually occurs in situations where capitation or daily rate payment systems are in operation.

Where, for example, a patient requires very intensive surgery, chemotherapy or dialysis, the provider claims a special payment from the social health insurance fund, based on an approved list of such treatments and therapies. Depending on the "generosity" of the capitation fee or the daily rate which is payable, some countries would have a wider or narrower list of treatments for which a special payment could be claimed.

The table below provides an overview of the different payment methods.

Overview of payment methods

Payment method	Description	Field of application	Remarks
Fee for service	Payment for each act or product provided	Outpatient and inpatient care, drugs	Problem is to contain costs
Per case	Payment per case, normally according to diagnosis	Outpatient specialist care, inpatient care	It is difficult to administer
Flat rate	Payment of lump sums for the coverage of certain costs	Investment	Is used in combination with other payment methods
Daily rate	Payment of a rate per day of treatment, which covers all costs or a large part of the costs	In patient care, long term care	Gives a strong incentive to extend the length of stay
Capitation	Payment per patient for a certain period covering all costs	Primary care and secondary care	Quality assurance needed
Budget	Payment of an amount which is supposed to cover all costs of the facility during a fixed period (a month, a year)	All kinds of facilities	Budget has to be adapted to utilization of facilities and development of prices of goods needed
Bonus	Payment of a certain amount for the achievement of objectives	Primary care, sometimes secondary care. Payment for remote posts	
Salary	Monthly salary payable to staff with employment contracts	Mostly in facilities owned by the health insurance	Other costs will have to be taken into account like investment costs and material for example
Special payments	Payable for expensive cases	Mostly in hospitals or in primary care	Should be limited to a pre-defined list of cases. Is very similar to per-case payments

Unit 2: Issues to consider

A. Choosing the right payment methods

Some systems have clear advantages over others with respect to one or more of the performance characteristics – cost containment, quality of services, and administration.

The different levels of health care provision – primary, secondary and tertiary – may all warrant a different approach to the payment of providers. A system of payment which may be entirely appropriate for primary care may simply not be feasible for tertiary care. There will be very few circumstances where one method is appropriate for paying providers of care at *all* levels.

It is not easy to choose between the systems and the most efficient systems for a given country will depend greatly on the local situation. If, however, the social health organization has the capability, it is wise to use a combination of payment methods at each level rather than be a prisoner to only one – particularly in the early stages of a scheme.

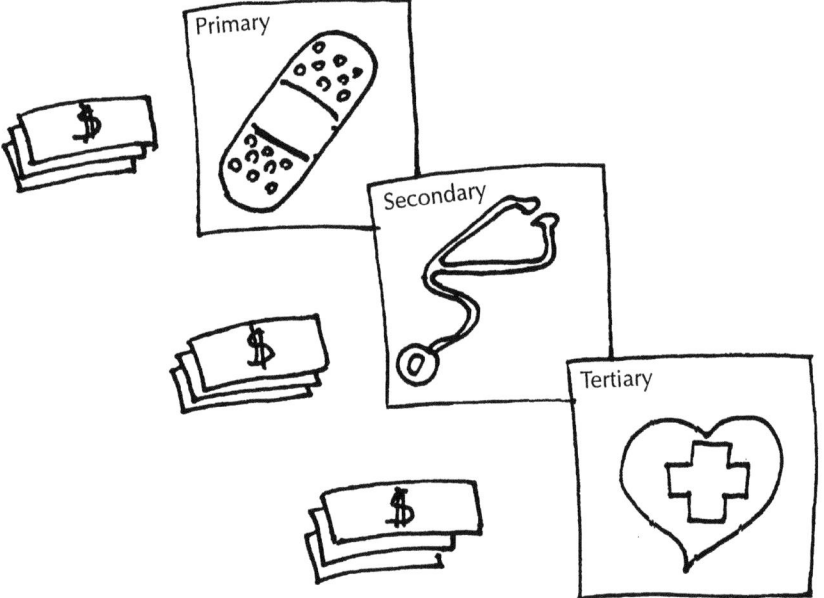

Fig. 12:
"... wise to use a combination of payment methods ... rather than be a prisoner to ... one ..."

B. Quality of care and cost containment

In terms of cost containment, both the budget and the capitation provider payment methods offer the most cost-effective payment mechanisms for social health insurance systems. Both systems are also relatively easy to administer. Where the providers are contractually obliged to provide care within a specified set of standards for a fixed annual payment, this offers a clear incentive for providers to give an economical and efficient service. However, the quality of the care provided *must* be monitored. Moreover, many factors – political, organizational, socio-cultural and logistical – impinge on making such an objective decision and the circumstances of the country must be taken into account before adopting one mechanism rather than another.

C. Administration

While both capitation and budget payment systems are relatively straightforward to administer, there is still a need – as with all of the other payment mechanisms – to clearly analyse costs of care so that reasonable rates can be set for providers. Determining the cost of health care is difficult enough in the OECD countries but is an even bigger challenge in developing countries. It is often the case that private insurance companies will have a more detailed understanding of costs than do public providers, since private companies are profit-oriented and therefore need to understand the financial margins within which they are operating. The Ministry of Health may have information about "block costs" of provider units and this information should be analysed carefully. If at all possible, information should also be sought from private providers and insurance companies as this will almost certainly give a more detailed breakdown of costs.

The administration which each of the payment methods involves also needs to be taken into account when deciding on the method to be adopted. Some of the payment mechanisms (e.g. fee-for-service and cost per case) require a large and qualified administration in order to receive, validate and pay claims, and to arbitrate on issues of contention between providers and the social health insurance organization. Other systems, such as capitation and budget payment, do not require the same numbers of administrative staff because claims for individual cases are only made in exceptional circumstances. Quality assurance programs *must*, however, be developed and implemented. In the capitation system the social health insurance organization requires details of patients registered with providers in order to pay those providers. In the case of budget payment, the amount to be paid is negotiated between the social health insurance organization and the providers, and is paid direct to the providers.

Bonus and flat-rate payment systems are also relatively easy to administer and are good in terms of cost containment. The salary system, however, is not strong on quality and is only regarded as fair on cost containment.

D. Which method – and when?

It is quite possible that different payment mechanisms will be adopted at different stages in the development, implementation and revision of a social health insurance scheme. For example, a flat-rate payment mechanism may be used during the period of commissioning of a new facility, subsequently changing to a cost per case system once the facility is in operation.

Equally (as already indicated) it is not unusual for two – or sometimes three – payment mechanisms to be in operation for the same types of services. For example, a capitation system may be in operation for primary care, with bonus payments being made if the doctor or facility meets or exceeds targets for particular services set by the social health insurance fund.

E. Political issues

The introduction of a new payment system has to take into account many political issues, which depend on the environment in the respective country. Issues that will certainly arise are:

- Which payment system are providers accustomed to in the country?

    (If for example providers are accustomed to charge fees and to negotiate these with the patients, they might resist new methods like capitation).

- Will it be possible to get providers for the terms of payment foreseen and is there an oversupply or a shortage of health care providers?

(If there is a shortage, the health insurance organization will find it difficult to impose a payment system on the existing providers).

- Will the new payment method reduce or increase the income of providers or will it change the distribution of income among certain provider groups or will it be neutral?

    (These are issues that certainly will be brought up form interested provider groups).

- Will it be possible to avoid additional "under the table payments"?

    (In many countries, where there are official payment methods in place, providers tend to improve their income by charging unofficial fees. It is a difficult task for health insurance to abolish such a practice).

- Will it be possible to implement quality assurance programs?

    (If per capita payment and budget systems are introduced, it is especially important that the quality of care provided must be monitored).

SOCIAL HEALTH INSURANCE

MODULE 6:
THE INSURANCE ORGANIZATION

International Labour Office   International Social Security Association

SOCIAL HEALTH INSURANCE

MODULE CONTENTS

Unit 1: **Organizational aspects**

    A. Legislation and regulation

    B. Registration of employers and employees

    C. Collection and recording of contributions

    D. Compliance

    E. Claims administration

    F. Benefits

    G. Provider management

    H. Financial management

Unit 2: **Contact with other agencies**

Ministry of Labour

Ministry of Health

Ministry of Education

Other Ministries

MODULE 6

THE INSURANCE ORGANIZATION

Unit 1: Organizational aspects

Introduction

There are many different ways in which health insurance may be organized but all options should take into account the need to meet certain requirements in order to achieve the objectives linked to the introduction of health insurance – these are:

- Health insurance needs to have financial accounts which are administered apart from the State budget.

  This is important because otherwise the health insurance contributions will simply be regarded as additional tax and the monies collected might well be used for other than health insurance purposes.

- This normally also implies the need for an independent management of the health insurance fund.

  The advantage of this is also that, to a certain extent, health insurance is then independent from political interference or "power play".

- Administrative flexibility can more easily be achieved if health insurance is independent from public regulations (e.g. relating to procedures for tendering, salary scales, and other formal arrangements).

- The separation of health insurance from public finance and policy also has the advantage of reducing the State's influence, thus enhancing pluralism and subsidiarity.

There are many options for the organization of health insurance as autonomous non-state bodies, some of which are as:

- a separate administration under an existing government ministry with a management appointed by the minister, but with separate accounts;

- an autonomous self-governing body under public legislation (the management may be appointed through elections or by social groups – e.g. trade unions and employers);

- a non-government organization (NGO) in which case the State hands over the responsibility to NGOs for the organization of health insurance (the state may, however, determine the rules);

- different funds which are competing for members (this model is chosen by more and more countries – for example, Russia, Slovakia and Germany).

In countries which have separate schemes for different groups – e.g. government employees, agriculture workers, specific enterprises or for the private sector – each scheme may take a different form from among those options.

The self-governing schemes may have board of directors and a supervisory board, consisting of representatives of government departments, workers and employers organizations – i.e. a "tripartite board". The board would be responsible for overall policy, constituting a form of public control, and also for co-ordinating between the health insurance scheme(s) and government agencies.

In developing countries, almost without exception, compulsory health insurance is first established as a semi-autonomous public agency or institution under a government department (often the Ministry of Health or Labour or Social Welfare).

Whatever the organizational and administrative arrangements, the social health insurance organization *must* be operated under legislation. That legislation should be drafted during the planning phase, be revised to incorporate policy developments, and then be submitted to the legislature for approval and enactment. All elements of the organization should be defined in the legislation but operational and administrative arrangements are normally excluded, usually being presented separately in regulations and operating instructions. If there is an existing social insurance structure which targets the same insured population, then the legislation for the social health insurance organization should be linked to it in order to avoid duplication of administrative structures.

Irrespective of whether or not social health insurance is the first of a series of social protection schemes, or a stand-alone organization – or indeed part of a wider social insurance organization – certain functions need to be included in the structure. As a minimum, these are:

- **Legislation and regulation**
- **Registration of employers, employees and the insured**
- **Contribution collection and recording**
- **Compliance**
- **Administration of claims**
- **Benefits**
- **Data collection and production of information**
- **Management of providers**
- **Financial management**

and each of these will be examined, in turn, in this Unit.[8]

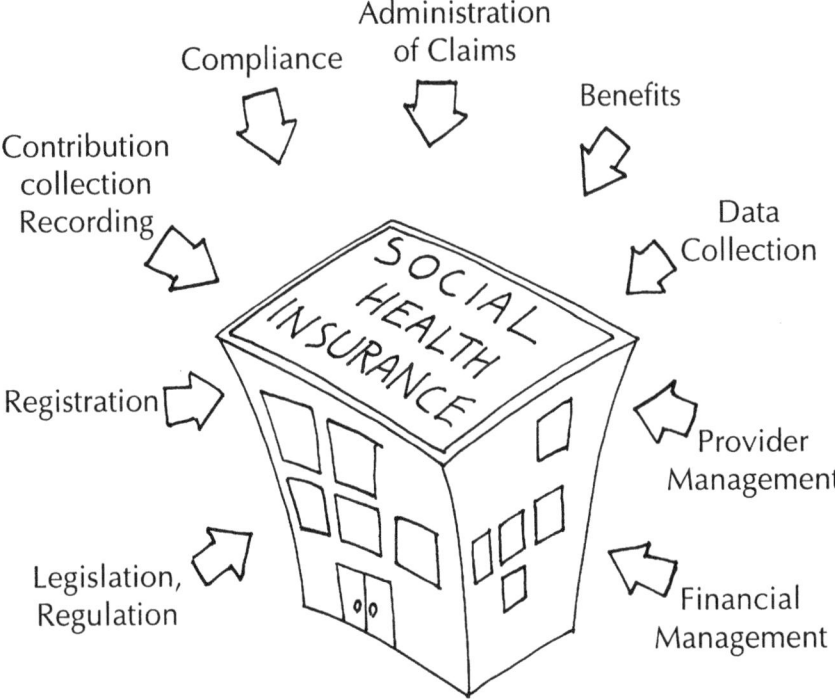

Fig. 13:
"... certain functions need to be included in the structure ...

---

[8] Note that a number of these topics are examined in some detail in the Manual "*Administration of Social Security*" which deals comprehensively with Registration (Module 2), Collection and Recording of Contributions (Module 3), Compliance and Enforcement (Module 4) and Award and payment of benefits (Module 5).

A. Legislation and regulation

There are several documents which might regulate the functioning of social health insurance, in particular these are:

- The basic laws;
- Government ordinances;
- The statutes of the health insurance fund;
- Guidelines and internal regulations of the health insurance
- Contracts with providers.

Different countries will make different decisions as to which issues are regulated by which documents. Nevertheless there are some elements which might serve as a distinction between different types of regulation. The following table provides an overview of these.

Instruments for regulating health insurance

Instrument	Field of application	Approved by	Example
Legislation	Determination of the basic rules of health insurance	Parliament	Membership, determination of contribution, constitution etc.
Government ordinances	To regulate details of functioning and issues which are subject to frequent changes	Government	Fee schedules, quality standards
Government approval	To approve certain decisions taken by the health insurance management	Government	Annual budget of the health insurance, contribution rate
Statutes of the fund	Terms or internal organization and responsibility	Board, government	Responsibility of organization (director general, board, supervising board etc.)
Guidelines	Administrative procedures	Management	Details of benefit approval, contribution collection procedures etc.
Contracts	Terms of health care provision	Management of health insurance and of providers	Payment of providers, utilization of forms etc.

It needs to be very clear which decisions should be resolved by laws and ordinances and which may be taken by other instruments. The range of decisions which will have to be taken will include:

- the general design of the health system;
- the regulation of technical details which may be subject to frequent changes;
- the terms of health care provisions;
- day to day decisions on the administration of health insurance.

The general design of the health system ...

... needs to be defined by law and the appropriate legislation should specify:

- all questions relating to membership and coverage;
- the organization, responsibilities and decision-making authority;
- the relationship with providers;
- the benefits provided by the health fund.

Other important features should be noted:

- the overall structure of the health insurance scheme should be laid down in a health insurance law
- details which may be subject to frequent change may be established in ordinances or regulations.

Decisions relating to contributions, investment, employment of staff, contracts with providers should be the responsibility of the health fund but approval by the Ministry of Health or Social Security may be needed for decisions concerning issues such as the annual budget or adjustment of contribution rates.

Day to day administrative procedures of the health insurance organization will be laid down in guidelines which standardize the practices and procedures of the health insurance organization's personnel and ensure that their decisions are reliable.

The drafting and defining of the legislative arrangements – both for the setting up of a health insurance organization and for continuing policy developments in the provisions of the organization – require skilled, qualified, and experienced staff.

The legislative document needs to include all of the elements which will enable the organization to function effectively, without constraining the operation of activities. The document should include at least the following elements:

- *The key features of the scheme -*
    - coverage of the scheme and dependency arrangements; eligibility; health benefits to be provided, financing, co-payments.

- *Arrangements for organization and decision-making*
    - including an overseeing body and its: establishment; constitution; conditions of service; committees; appointments.

- *Provider payment arrangements*
    - specifically the type of payments authorised to be made by the insurance institution.

B. Registration of employers and employees

Employers who are required to be registered with the social health insurance institution will be determined by the legislation. In some countries it is administratively easier to include employer groups progressively, for example beginning with those with a specified larger number of employees and gradually including those with fewer employees until all employers are registered.

Basically there are several categories of employers, each of which has specific requirements concerning registration and later contribution assessment. The following table gives an overview of the types of employers and of the special problems linked with their registration.

Registration of employers and employees in different types of enterprises

Employers	Special features	Problems	Solutions
Public employers	• Public administration, public enterprises	• Often accustomed to special benefits and therefore not interested in social health insurance • Budget problems of public employers	• Special regulations for public employers
Large industrial and service enterprises	• More than 100 employees	• High fluctuations of employees • Sophisticated strategies to avoid contributions	• Close contact and co-operation with the enterprises • Monitoring • Co-operation with tax offices
Small and medium service, crafts, trade and industrial enterprises	• Medium: 100 and less employees • Small: 10 and less	• Often informal employments • Temporary contracts • Contracts on the basis of "self-employment" • No registration • No staff record and bookkeeping	• Personal contact • Control by visits
Large enterprises in agriculture	• More than 100 employees • Agriculture, forestry and fishing	• Seasonal employment • Informal employment relations • Workers have no permanent address • Large regional distribution • Illiterate and unskilled, easy to replace • Unstable employment	• Control by visits
Small and medium enterprises in Agriculture	• Medium: 100 and less than 100 • Small: 10 and less employees • Agriculture, forestry and fishing	• Seasonal employment • Informal employment relations • Workers have no permanent address • Large regional distribution • Illiterate and unskilled	• Control by visits

In most countries, businesses need to be licensed in order to operate. It can be made a condition of the granting of a licence that the employer *is* registered with the social health insurance institution. This makes enforcement of the scheme much easier for that institution.

There are various sources from which social health insurance organizations may obtain information about existing employers in order to contact and register these, for example:

- membership data of the Chamber of Commerce,
- Tax authority data
- Business registration data.

It is usually the responsibility of – and a requirement for – the employer to inform the social health insurance institution of *all* employees and to provide updates on new employees and those leaving (referred to as "starters and leavers"). The definition of "an employee" must be included in the legislation and enforced by the social health insurance inspectors.

Often employers try to limit or reduce their financial liability to employees

- by registering them as "trainees" rather than as full employees,
- by remunerating with a small basic payment plus several additional allowances (and paying contributions only on the basic) or
- by retaining workers on a series of short-term contracts – with short breaks between each – in order to avoid paying contributions on their behalf.

Some enterprises will go to great lengths in order to avoid meeting the contribution liability for their employees. While it is often argued that it is the small enterprises which initially suffer from the requirement to comply with social health insurance institutions, it is quite often the very large organizations which invest in mechanisms to avoid compliance.

Many social health insurance schemes provide coverage for dependants in addition to the contributors to the scheme. The registration of dependants is normally not possible via the employer. As the registration of dependants is a very difficult operation, it is wise to develop mechanisms which obviate the need for *each* dependant to be separately registered. Depending on local conditions, health facilities, provider arrangements and numbers of dependants covered, a system of verification of entitlement needs to be developed, either by way of incorporating the names and national identity numbers of family members on the contributor's membership card or by some other acceptable means.

C. Collection and recording of contributions

As mentioned earlier in the manual, this is one of the topics which is extensively dealt with in the *Administration Manual* and, for this reason, only those issues which are particularly relevant to health insurance contributions are referred to here.

As with registration, contribution collection is more or less difficult according to kind, size of enterprise and type of workers.

This is why in many countries very different ways of contribution payment and collection may be found, including:

- monthly, quarterly or yearly payment;
- payment by bank transfer, cash or even in kind;
- payment to social health insurance agencies or to other agencies (e.g. banks, post offices).

For larger, especially industrial, enterprises and in urban environments, even in developing countries it is usual for employers to make monthly payments to the scheme, which include their own contributions on behalf of their employees together with the employees' contributions. Many health insurance schemes impose an automatic fine or penalty on the employer if payment is not received by the due date. For enterprises which experience economic difficulties, the health insurance organization will sometimes permit payment to be made by instalments.

Frequently, health insurance institutions establish arrangements with approved agents for the collection of contributions. The agents available to be used in this way vary according to the level of infra-structural development in a country but might include banks, post offices, local health insurance offices or perhaps a combination of these. The advantage of having collection arrangements which are operated via banks and post offices is that they are often the only organizations which have a country-wide network of offices and therefore provide relatively easy access for most employers. Making use of these synergy options is a question of cost-effectiveness for the health insurance organization.

Where other social protection arrangements are already in place, which involve the collection of contributions from the same target population covered by the health insurance scheme, arrangements for collection of contributions for all schemes should be merged. Agents acting for the institution(s) normally receive a percentage of the total amount collected, in return for undertaking the task.

The amount to be paid to the agent should be negotiated and agreed in advance of the scheme's start date and the arrangements should be explicit. The social health insurance institution should resist any attempt to make arrangements which would limit the ability to operate effectively, for example agreeing to pay a minimal percentage of the contributions to the agent in return for enabling that agent to undertake all the recording and banking arrangements. Depending on the size of the target population, acting as an agent and collecting contributions for a social health insurance institution can be a very lucrative business. The potential for the agent to realize an early profit and to benefit from spin-off arrangements (for example business and/or private individuals opening accounts with the agency bank) should not be underestimated by the social health insurance institution when negotiating with the agent about payment for the service.

The agent deposits the payment in the social health insurance institution's account and payments should be accompanied by identification of the enterprises and the insured by or for whom the payments were made. It is the task of the collecting agent to establish this information. It is normally then the task of the health insurance institution to compare these data with the register and to check that the payments match with the contributions due.

The health insurance administration should define standard data requirements, forms to be used, and payment procedures. The basis for the assessment of the contributions to be paid by the enterprises is the staff record and accounts and it is the staff record documents which enables the health insurance institution to verify identity of the insured. The accounts record is the basis for verification of salaries and the declared contributions.

In many countries neither of these two items of information is available and in this case it is the task of the insurance institution to develop techniques which enable it to obtain the required information; these might be:

- visiting the enterprises and estimating salaries;

- approaching the enterprise via the staff member and his/her family.

The need for such action normally arises at the time when an individual becomes ill and needs health care services and at that point there is a need to check whether the individual has been registered, where they work and whether contributions have been paid.

It is important that the legislation makes clear that the responsibility for payment of any unpaid contributions to the health insurance fund is the enterprise – *not* the employee.

D. Compliance

It is one of the main tasks of the administration of social health insurance to ensure compliance with the scheme's legislation – in particular with the requirements to register and pay contributions. It is usual to have specially trained staff members who have the task of

- maintaining contacts with employers
- verifying information provided by employers
- enforcing the payment of contributions
- negotiating payment by instalments, if necessary.

The agents responsible for contacting enterprises should be qualified to provide assistance to them, for example in legal issues linked to social health insurance and other social security issues.

In many countries, health insurance administrations are equipped with special powers, in order to enforce contribution collection, which enable them to :

- seize bank accounts,
- distrain assets.

If the administration is not equipped with such rights, courts need to become involved and this makes the procedures more expensive and time consuming.

In any event, health insurance agents should have access to all relevant documents and records. They may, for example, need to

- check the number of employees actually *working* at any one time;
- compare this with the number of employees *registered* with the social health insurance organization;
- examine records of the payments made to staff in order to ensure that employees are not being denied their rights under the health insurance legislation;
- ensure that appropriate amounts *are* being contributed to the social health insurance fund.

The legislation should also make provision for the prosecution of any employer who fails to register or to comply with the requirement to pay health insurance contributions.

Special measures are needed to deal with cases of insolvency, liquidation or bankruptcy, primarily so that employees are protected and are not denied entitlements because of the employer's non-payment of contributions to the heath insurance scheme.

E. Claims administration

Claims processing involves a number of activities which are necessary in order to keep pace with payments, check entitlements and control costs. Those activities include:

- verification of entitlement, by the patient, to social health insurance benefits (either as a member or as a dependant);
- verification that the services provided are covered by the health insurance scheme
- verifying that the prices and fees are in accordance with regulations and contracts (if they exist);
- registering the claim;
- calculating possible co-payments for the patient;
- initiating payment of the claim;
- recording the payment.

Clearly, a large part of these activities can be automated, if computerised systems are available. It is also possible to reduce administration costs by formalizing data exchange with providers and it should be remembered that the quality of claims processing has an important influence on the overall costs of the insurance scheme.

F. Benefits

With health insurance benefits, the task of the health insurance administration consists mainly of services to insured members, for example by providing:

- information about entitlements and services
- information about available providers
- assistance with the processing of applications for certain benefits which need approval.

These services normally require some degree of personal contact between the insurance organization and the insured and, to this end, various models have been elaborated and tested which all have the objective of ensuring that there is a facility for that personal contact, for example:

- in countries where the infrastructure is well developed, most of those contacts may be made over the telephone or through the mail;
- there are also countries where the health insurance organization maintains regional (or even local) offices;
- health insurance organizations can locate some of their clerks in main provider institutions – e.g. hospitals or polyclinics.

Administrative requirements in the field of benefits will clearly increase with the volume and variety of benefits provided. If the scheme benefits consist of only basic primary care and, perhaps, basic inpatient services then benefit administration will require relatively little attention. If, however, the benefit package is more sophisticated (and especially if approvals for certain benefits are required) the administration will be far more labour intensive.

G. Provider management

Provider management refers to the core of health insurance – to the organization, monitoring and payment of health care services. The role of provider management is wide ranging and includes:

- establishing and applying criteria for accreditation of providers;
- defining, drawing up and monitoring contracts with providers;
- applying and monitoring a quality assurance programme;
- ensuring that beneficiaries have the information and advice which they need in order to choose an approved provide;.
- paying the providers. (This may be done as already explained in the section dealing with "claims processing" but it may also involve payment of capitation fees which need completely different administrative procedures).

In addition to the range of activities described above, it is also essential to have information and advice available for potential providers and for those who wish to join the approved list of providers. It is also important to ensure that a balance is

H. Financial management

The most difficult task in the financial management of health insurance is the management of cash flow and reserves. The smaller the fund the more difficult this is – especially as the cost of health services increases. For the smaller funds, this implies the necessity to maintain a reserve in order to cope with significant changes in cash flow.

Reserves

In the social security field there are two main types of reserves, *technical* and *contingency*.

- *Technical reserves* are those which are held against future liabilities and which, at the same time, play a part in financing the cost of benefits by generating investment income.

- *Contingency reserves* are those which are held to meet any temporary insufficiency arising out of a shortfall of contribution income or an excess of benefit expenditure.

Technical reserves are generally associated with long-term benefits, including pensions payable in respect of permanent disability or death. Contingency reserves are generally associated with the financing of short-term benefits, such as health care.

In social health insurance, it is usual to maintain a contingency reserve at a level equivalent to at least two months operating costs. However, this should be at a higher level if the coverage of the scheme is low, and marginally lower if the coverage of the scheme is high and the risks are spread wider. When a social health insurance fund first starts up it is advisable to maintain a larger contingency reserve and reduce it only when the expenditure stabilizes.

Legislation should normally prescribe the areas of investment appropriate for reserves so that effective security of the funds can be guaranteed. Investments are normally restricted to national outlets, if not by social health insurance legislation then by national legislation or local conventions or circumstances. Investments are also subject to the approval of the appropriate Minister in consultation with the Minister of Finance. Within the context of health care, small amounts of reserves are often invested in specific health-related activities – such as clinics, rehabilitation units and prosthetic development.

Safety, liquidity, yield

The legislation or regulations governing investments should have regard to the importance of safety, yield, and liquidity.

Safety of investments indicates the certainty of recovery of the invested capital and of the yield on that capital. With respect to inflation, for example, safety of investment means the maintenance of the real value of invested sums. Most social health insurance schemes do not prescribe a required minimum yield but must ensure the best possible yield for the investment. It is clearly good business practice to protect the value of the funds and, where possible, increase them.

Yield on investment is measurable and demands a high priority when determining the choice of investment. However, yield must also be balanced with safety and liquidity depending on the stability of the health fund.

Liquidity refers to the ease and speed with which investments may be turned into operating cash. For short-term benefits, such as social health insurance, liquidity of investments is important. Improvements in the provision of health care almost inevitably create an inflationary spiral in the total cost of health care, through raised expectations of beneficiaries and the rising cost of staff and equipment.

(More detailed reference to investment of funds is made in Module 4 of the manual on Social Security Financing[9]).

In most social heath insurance funds, responsibility for decisions about the investment of funds rests with a tripartite management board, which is subject to control by the supervisory authority.

Clarification of responsibilities

In order to provide maximum security for the fund (i.e. the monies collected through compulsory contributions) a clear internal distribution of responsibilities and of supervision is necessary. The regulations must make clear

- who will be entitled to dispose of the funds of the insurance scheme,
- how decisions are taken and documented,
- who will be entitled to sign cheques, bank transfers and
- who is permitted to dispose of the cash resources of the fund

and corresponding procedures, security regulations and supervision must also be regulated.

---

9   Social Security Financing – (Manual No. 3 in this series) – ISBN 92-2-110736-1

Accounting

The accounting function deserves particular emphasis for it is accounting and frequent reporting which form the basis for planning, efficient administration, control and cost containment.

Accounting is the recording of *all* financial movements into or out of the social health insurance fund's accounts. It should reflect *all* financial resources by way of contributions, interest, and any other income, as well as *all* financial commitments including payment of providers and administration costs (including the institution's own staff and all agency fees). A simplified, illustrative, financial picture is presented below.

INCOME	EXPENDITURE
• Contributions • Interest from capital investments • Other income (rent, sale of old equipment, subsidies, reimbursements, refunds, etc.)	• Providers • Administration
ASSETS	LIABILITIES
• Real Estate • Security holdings, bank accounts • Other assets (equipment, vehicles, materials, etc.).	• Capital • Reserves • Bank credits • Unpaid invoices & vouchers

(The table is adapted from *Social Health Insurance: A Guidebook for Planning* (page 100) – a World Health Organization publication developed as a cooperative initiative of the ILO and WHO).

More sophisticated analytical accounting systems allow not only documented financial flows but also the correct assignment of costs to specific headings – e.g. time periods, individual departments, specific activities, etc..

The accounting system *must* be accompanied by an efficient information system, for the two systems go very much hand in hand. It should also be very carefully designed because any subsequent changes will affect the ability to compare figures for different years and will also require, for computerized systems, expensive software amendments.

Unit 2: Contact with other agencies

Introduction

The development of health insurance will affect

- other areas of policy,
- the feasibility of other taxes and charges and
- the government's objectives.

If social health insurance is to be successful, these effects must be anticipated and taken into account in the planning of the system.

In the course of planning, implementing or revising a social health insurance system, therefore, the social health insurance institution will need to establish and maintain contact with numerous government ministries and with those external agencies which have an interest in the country's health care programme. Some of the contacts will be informal, others will be formal, particularly those with certain ministries.

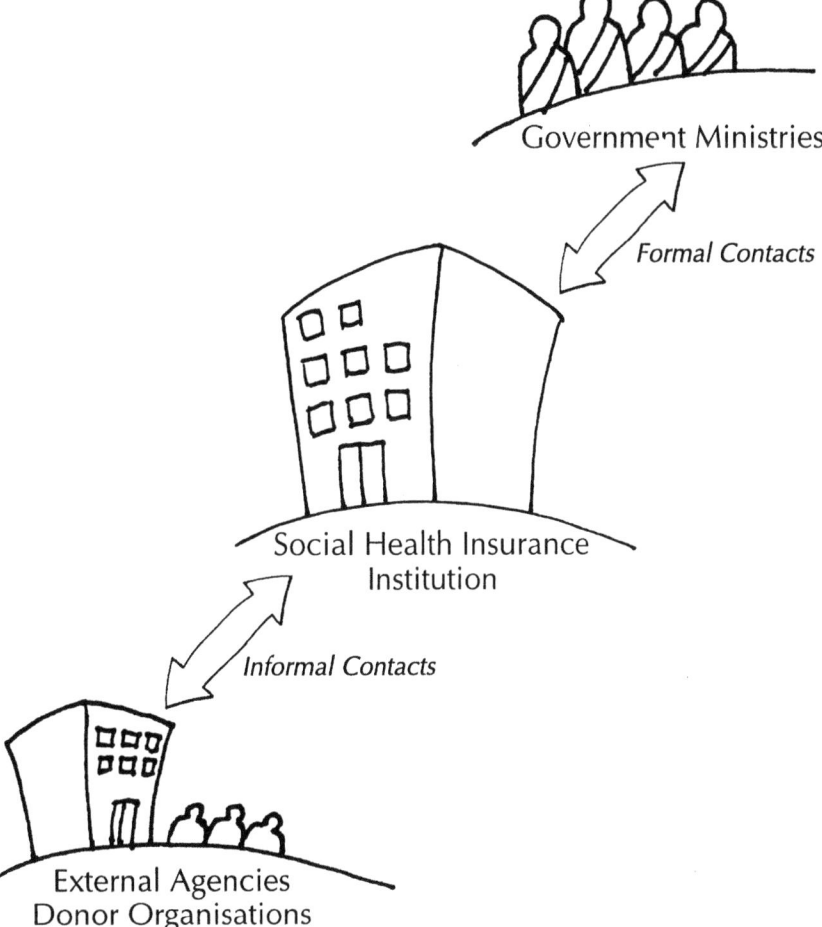

Fig. 14:
"...establish and maintain contact with ... government ministries ... and ... external agencies ..."

The Ministry of Labour

The Ministry under whose aegis the social health insurance scheme operates is often the Ministry of Labour. This is because that Ministry is usually the one which has responsibility for the development and implementation of social protection measures for employed persons – and thus for social security schemes. Social health insurance schemes are often implemented as part of a wider social security or social protection programme. In some countries the Ministry has wider responsibilities than labour and is sometimes vested with responsibilities for both labour *and* welfare.

Ministry of Health

Planning, implementation or revision of a social health insurance scheme requires regular and detailed collaboration with the Ministry of Health. In countries with an established social health insurance scheme, there will often be a designated department within that Ministry which deals specifically with issues relating to the scheme. In many countries, the Ministry's Planning Department is the focal point. It is also likely that other departments will feature in discussions, notably departments dealing with registration of doctors, registration of non-public health facilities, the public health department, and the information and statistics department. It is normally the latter which analyses and disseminates information on clinical activity and utilization of health services.

Ministry of Education

The Ministry of Education is sometimes responsible for undergraduate medical education and for the training of nursing and laboratory staff. Where advice is needed on the types of clinical education available, or where changes to curricula are warranted due to changing needs of the health services, the Ministry of Education should be consulted.

Ministry of Education staff, including all teachers, are usually included in the schemes which provide health cover to civil servants.

Other Ministries

Other Ministries which could be relevant to social health insurance are:

- Ministry of Defence

    (Often the armed forces have their own health insurance arrangements)

- Ministry of Interior Affairs (see Ministry of Defence)

- Ministry of Finance

    (In countries where there are transfers from the State budget to the health insurance fund or where the tax authorities collect health insurance contributions)

- Ministry of Justice

    (Where questions arise about reinforcement of contribution collection)

Fields of cooperation

Fields of cooperation between different ministries and the social health insurance institution are multiple, for example:

- Legislation -

    Health insurance may co-operate with the responsible ministries in the question of drafting legislation.

- Supervision -

    Either the Ministry of Labour or the Ministry of Health normally have the task of supervising social health insurance. This includes the approval of the budget and of the contribution rate.

- Health policy -

    Health insurance may support the responsible ministries in the implementation of health programs.

- Statistics -

    Health insurance may support the ministries in the elaboration and provision of data for basic statistics.

- Contribution collection and registration -

    Ministries may assist the social health insurance organization in fields such as data for registration, reinforcement of contribution collection, etc.

External agencies

Most developing countries have a number of external agencies which are involved in project activities, or in the investment of financial or human resources, aimed at encouraging and assisting development. In the health sector these activities can range from local, community-based projects, through national programmes for health education or immunization and vaccination, to investment in establishing a complete health system. Much empirical data will normally be available from such agencies and, more importantly, their information about health needs is usually up-to-date.

Most of the main international organizations will each have an office in the capital of each developing country. The health or social security advisers in these offices should be approached, in the first instance, for advice and assistance. Some of the non-governmental organizations (NGOs) and religious organizations which provide health care will also be a source of up-to-date information and relevant advice and will have detailed information on locality-based health needs. It is often useful to include NGO representatives in early planning meetings on social health insurance even though their experience is usually limited to particular individual localities or to specific health programmes.

SOCIAL HEALTH INSURANCE

MODULE 7: INFORMATION SYSTEMS

International Labour Office — International Social Security Association

MODULE CONTENTS

Unit 1: **Internal information**

Unit 2: **External Information**

SOCIAL HEALTH INSURANCE

MODULE 7

INFORMATION SYSTEMS

Unit 1: Internal information

Although the unit is concerned primarily with the information requirements of the institution responsible for the operation of the health insurance scheme, it should be remembered that information is important to those on each side of the health insurance system – not only those running the health scheme and providing the services and benefits, but also the scheme's members.

Fig. 15:
"... information is important to those ... running the scheme ... providing services and benefits ... and the scheme's members ..."

This unit will therefore examine the information needed by the fund organizers and unit two will look at the importance of information to those outside the health insurance organization.

In the case of the health fund's managers, the focus needs to be on information required in order to run the scheme successfully; in the case of the scheme's members, consideration will be given to what information they may require in order to make the scheme more understandable, accessible and transparent.

Operational information requirements

The point has already been made – but is well worth repeating – that good statistical information provides the basis for planning and control. This philosophy is widely and readily recognized and accepted in countries with well developed health insurance schemes. However, in many developing countries, the introduction into the health services of an efficient, business-like information system is a new concept, can be a frightening prospect, and is often resisted by those most likely to benefit from it. Resistance tends to be based on "fear of the unknown" or a fear of exposure to new decision-making tools which are logical, rational or scientifically based.

However, once users are persuaded of the applications and benefits of a robust information system, they usually – if tentatively at the outset – accept the challenge of participating in the development of such a system.

Basic principles

There are a number of basic principles to be borne in mind when developing such a system, in order to ensure that the implementation is as successful possible

Sophisticated computerization, although not an essential ingredient for a useful information system, is clearly desirable and not only considerably speeds up the administrative process but also offers a much wider range of outputs than is readily available from manually operated systems. Nevertheless, a manual information system *can* be sufficiently effective, particularly if the system users identify the *essential* information requirements and fully understand and apply the outputs.

Defining information needs

If the process of identifying and analysing information needs is to be of use to the key players – and to the organization – it is much more important that facilitators have a sound understanding of how social health insurance organizations operate than it is for them to understand computers. Computers are simply the tools which assist analytical tasks: the information needs of an organization should *not* be made to fit a preconceived computer system.

Consultation with potential users

Potential users of an information system must therefore be consulted so that they can help identify and clarify their information requirements. During the consultation process it often becomes clear that decisions made in the past have been based on little or no concrete information but rather on "gut reaction". Whilst such reaction *may* be fairly reliable for those with long experience (and may indeed often be fairly accurate) in order to make *informed* management and planning decisions, a robust information system – where the information is accepted by *all* the users – will prove more convincing.

It is important to recognize that any information system must reflect the capacity of the institutions involved to

- collect and collate the base data
- assess and analyse that data and
- present the analyses in the form of comprehensible information which can be used for management and planning purposes.

The different stages involved in processing or "converting" data into information relate to different departments and divisions within a social health insurance scheme. There needs to be a clear indication of relative responsibilities in terms of data collection, collation, analysis, and presentation of information to users. The success of the information system depends on the capacity of each of the responsible sections to meet their respective responsibilities.

Potential users at the operational level of a social health insurance scheme – the care providers – must be able to see the *immediate* relevance of the information before their support, in ensuring accurate data collection, can be guaranteed.

It is far more likely that information will be both accepted and usable if the same base data is used to feed the information needs of operational managers as well as the strategic levels of health care management and planning. By using the same base data for *all* analyses, one organizational level of the organization cannot accuse another of concocting or inventing information to suit its own purposes. For the base data to be comparable across and within levels (for example between providers) definitions of the data elements must be explicit and be understood by those who collect data, collate that data, analyse and use it.

Analysis of process

The first step towards determining information requirements is an analysis of the administrative process – particularly in terms of the flow of information – and this involves obtaining answers to the following questions:

- who needs information
- what information is needed
- when is it needed
- from which source(s) will it be obtained.

On the basis of the analysis, forms, processes, databases and possible software solutions may be developed.

User consultation

At each stage in the discussion, the user should be asked what information is required to make decisions and what information therefore needs to be available. This process should be repeated for all key players at each level and the process should be facilitated carefully.

Few managers will readily admit to a "seat of the pants" style of decision making. The purpose of undergoing the process referred to in the previous paragraph is to discover the sort of decisions which are made – in whatever way they are made – and what information the manager wishes to have available in that decision making process.

Consolidating information requirements

When the discussions are complete, those individuals from the social health insurance scheme who are responsible for identifying information requirements should then *consolidate* the information needs at *each* level.

Some information requirements will be identified by several users – indeed possibly by all of the users. Others will be identified only by a few users, or possibly only by one. The former does not actually mean that *each person* needs that information element, only that they are familiar with having that information and feel comfortable with it. Similarly, the latter should not mean that the information element identified by only one user should be excluded from the composite information requirements for that level. It may well be the case that individuals with very specific tasks will have a specific information requirement. What is important is that the composite information picture for that level is accepted and "owned" by the group of potential users. It may take a number of meetings with key players at each level before agreement is reached on the core information requirements.

Depending on the organization's infrastructure, this exercise could demand an inordinate amount of time, which the project timetable may not afford. In some countries, where health information is used and applied as a recognized feature of management and planning, this exercise has been known to take a full six months to complete (with the use of a team of external experts) for *one tier* of management.

A less thorough, but still very effective, method is for the individuals from the social health insurance team to identify the roles of each of the key players and set out the anticipated information requirements in advance of holding meetings with each of these individuals. Using an "outline of information requirements" as a guide and, possibly, presenting a set of sample output forms is a good way of generating debate on the individual information requirements. For those who are less confident of their roles, it may be tempting to accept the suggested output forms without question – but it would be foolish to do so. Lists of information requirements and proposed output forms should be used to facilitate discussion and debate and so elicit the *real* information requirements. It is also useful to get the full team of players together, at each level, to discuss their information requirements: at this point it often becomes clear that at least two individuals consider themselves to have responsibility for the same tasks. This is a useful forum in which to clarify those roles.

Unit 2: External information

During the planning phase it is essential that *all* relevant groups are kept well informed and that they are fully involved in discussions and consultation before plans are implemented. If such groups feel that they *have* participated in the planning process it is less likely that they will subsequently raise objections.

It is also important that the plans for the new system are well publicized and open to debate. Before new legislation comes into force, there should be an information campaign[10] to ensure that all members are aware of their responsibilities and, equally if not more importantly, that they are aware of the advantages which the new scheme will provide for them.

During the start-up period in particular, providing information and ensuring transparency should, hopefully, make the new health insurance system much more acceptable to members. It should be remembered, however, that informing the membership does not begin and end with the completion of the introductory phase of the new scheme. Keeping the membership informed must be an *ongoing* activity. One element of that activity is the need for the health insurance organization to have an information policy which regularly publicizes (for example) its own regulations, choice and accreditation and appointment of providers, periodic opportunities to change doctors under a capitation system, etc..

The impact of a social health insurance scheme

It should also be remembered that the development of social health insurance is likely to affect the interests of *many* groups within the population, for example:

- *employers* .... because they may have to pay contributions;
- em*ployees* .... because membership is likely to be compulsory and contributions will be deducted from their pay;
- *trade unions* .... because the interests of their members are affected (and possibly also because they will not wish to lose their influence over any labour issue);
- *health care providers* .... because they may be subject to payment regulations and quality control;

---

10 Brief reference is made to information campaigns in the manual *Administration of Social Security* (Module 6 Unit 2) which has been referred to several times throughout this manual.

- *existing organizations* (e.g. health insurance schemes, private insurance, etc.) .... because they may fear abolition or loss of clients;
- *government ministries* ... (e.g. the Agriculture Ministry may be responsible for social security for farmers; the Finance Ministry for deductions of various kinds; the Labour Ministry for social security; the Health Ministry for health policy, infrastructure, etc.; the Internal Affairs Ministry for public hospitals; etc.).

It is vital that, when developing plans for a health insurance scheme, the planners are aware of the groups and of their interests – and apprehensions – and also of the fact that a lack of consensus and support for the new scheme may have a negative effect on its success.

Proactive use of information

The manual began by looking at the role of social health insurance and it is appropriate, in this module, to provide a reminder of the advantages which need to be brought to the attention of members.

In addition to the more general advantages which have been referred to throughout the manual, it is perhaps worth emphasizing some of the specific benefits to be gained by the relevant interest groups and it is useful to point these out to those groups so as to ensure that the social health insurance scheme receives the broadest possible support from the outset. Those benefits include:

- the possibility that employers may see improvements in productivity because of the improved health status of their employees;
- the fact that scheme members and their families will have access to health care;
- the potential advantage for groups which already have some form of health insurance who will keep their own systems but may also have the right to buy complementary protection;
- for representatives of trade unions and employer organizations, that they may – indeed should – be able to participate in the administration of the health scheme;
- the fact that providers and related industries will have additional (and more reliable) income; the majority will be better off under social health insurance because greater financial resources will be available;
- the advantage for providers who will usually receive their remuneration directly from the health insurance funds, which will increase the reliability of payments;

- greater opportunities for additional training for those working in the health scheme;

- government interest in the scheme's effect on employment; for example, a scheme with 10 million members may well require 10,000 health service employees and yet more staff will be needed in hospitals, doctor's practices and in other provider units;

- advantages for provincial and local government which should benefit from infra structural improvement, through the building of hospitals and other provider units.

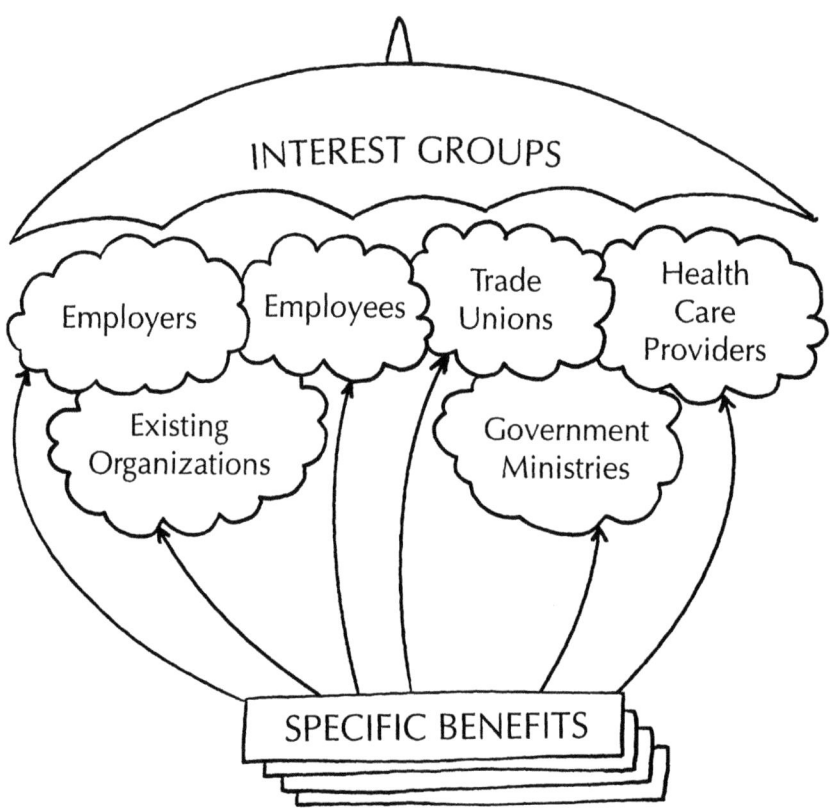

Fig. 16:
"... worth emphasizing ... benefits to be gained by ... interest groups ..."

SOCIAL HEALTH INSURANCE

MODULE 8:
A PRIMER ON MICRO-INSURANCE

International Labour Office   International Social Security Association

MODULE CONTENTS

Unit 1: What is *Micro-Insurance*?

Unit 2: Main features

Unit 3: Micro-Insurance as an alternative

SOCIAL HEALTH INSURANCE

MODULE 8

A PRIMER ON MICRO-INSURANCE

Unit 1: What is *Micro-Insurance?*

Recently, a concept has been introduced into the discussion about protection of vulnerable and excluded population groups – *Micro-Insurance*[11]. It is based on the experience that in many countries – especially developing countries – there are groups which, despite the existing social protection mechanisms, remain excluded from basic services such as health care.

Micro-insurance does not pretend to be *the* solution to this problem but it aims at integrating certain types of solution within a concept that focuses on action at grass-roots level.

"*Micro*" refers to the level of society at which the interaction is located that is smaller than national schemes; "*insurance*" refers to the economic instrument to be used. A more accurate description of the concept might be *voluntary group self-help schemes for social health insurance.*

The underpinning of micro-insurance is that, hitherto, excluded populations have not been covered under existing health insurance schemes because of several concurrent forces, such as:

- politicians and insurers have done too little to include these population segments;
- excluded people have forgone claiming access because of their dis-empowerment within society;
- there is a lack of resources;

---

[11] The following paragraphs are based on Dror, D; Jaquier, Ch: Micro-Insurance. Extending Health Insurance to the Excluded. International Social Security Review, ISSA, Vol. 52, N° 1, January-March 1999 P. 71-97.

- many people argue that it would be too difficult to include these groups into traditional social security schemes.

Micro-insurance proposes to change this situation by basing its activity on the following assumptions:

- **Demand-driven**

    To be attractive to excluded populations, micro-insurance must offer coverage for the most critical risks. As these differ according to peoples' living and working conditions, which are usually area- or trade-specific, the insurance must be adapted to specific conditions.

- **Empowerment**

    Effective adaptation can occur through a process of mediation composed of two essential functions – *empowerment* and *increased social capital*. The first comes about by enabling the population to express its own needs and priorities and the second by making public opinion more receptive to insurance.

- **Synergy**

    Even the most successful local micro-insurance unit will need to be bound with others to have the critical mass to develop into fully-fledged insurance. The mechanism for this aggregation will need to be elaborated, bearing in mind that it must also favour solidarity and equity.

Despite the small size of each unit, micro-insurance justifies being characterised as *insurance* and should not be confused with credit facilities or savings accounts. The main difference is that a savings account is an *intra*-personal inter-temporal trade (of current consumption for future consumption by the same person) whereas insurance is an *inter*-personal trade (from one group to another) or trade across states-of-nature.

Micro-insurance builds upon principles of insurance and applies them at local, community level. Thus it provides more solidarity, risk pooling and proper risk management than Medical Savings Accounts (MSA) or user fees. The risk pooling ability of micro-insurance depends on the size of the groups covered and how various schemes operate together. It allows the shift of payments for services over time and can be expected to be more transparent and easier to operate than national schemes.

Voluntary Membership

Affiliation to micro-insurance is voluntary and it is therefore important to understand what motivates an individual to join. The underlying economic motivation for joining a micro-insurance unit is assumed to be a desire

- to reduce the individual risk emerging from possible health costs or, more likely

- to have access to health care for an affordable contribution and
- to improve health status by controlling living and working conditions.

A second key motive relates to social affiliation. People do *not* live or work in isolation; on the contrary, they have a deep-rooted need to seek voluntary and repeated interaction with others. Those who have a formal employment relationship transfer part of their attachments from the family and the immediate wider community to the workplace – in return for the rewards gained through stable employment. However, the excluded population frequently cannot do so because of lack of access to a stable workplace and to the social protection that is available through it. They seek support in alternative structures, which can be geographic, occupational or social.

There is a hypothesis that outside pressures enhance group cohesion. Applying this hypothesis to populations which face several unfavourable conditions, we deduce that members may also join micro-insurance in response to group cohesion or pressure.

Risks covered

The next key characteristic of micro-insurance is the choice of risks that are covered. In general terms two prevalent approaches prevail:

- on the one hand, high-cost and low incidence "catastrophic" events (such as treatment for snake bites, emergency treatment of delivery complications, some cases of hospitalization);
- on the other hand, non-random, low cost events resembling primary care (including drugs, laboratory, supplementary care beyond that provided by government).

This two-pronged approach implies that, at least at the outset, there is no standard model for design of the benefit package. Granted, the package may change, depending mostly on the amount of accumulated reserves and the community-specific perception of priority risks/benefits. In this respect, micro-insurance units differ greatly from private, profit motivated insurances which modify the benefit package to improve profit (and/or increase market share) as well as from social insurance which focuses on a heterogeneous population and which is oriented towards bio-medical services.

The process of deciding on the risks that should be covered concentrates on social needs in contrast to the medical approach (which concentrates on health services) prevalent among most other insurances and other community-based experiments. Popular involvement in the definition of needs is important in that it enhances people's willingness to adhere to the system and to pay for community-defined needs (rather than only for individually-defined needs). As such, micro-insurance contributes to and is enhanced by community-building.

This also means that anyone who is not a member of the group would normally be excluded from the decision-making process, including medical staff. In principle, local health workers (nurse, midwife, first-aid volunteer, traditional healer, etc.) *can* take part in the decisions – provided they join the micro-insurance scheme. This, too, sets micro-insurance apart from traditional health insurances (both private and social) in that experts from outside the group can at best have a consultative position.

Micro-insurance is structured to harness group-dynamics in order to link individual economic motives with collective social responsibility, through a process of autonomous decision-making.

Micro-insurance units are conceived to be group-based, without assuming a romantic view of group life and it can function even in communities that do not demonstrate a high level of harmony. It is simply assumed that the joint economic activity of belonging to the same insurance scheme may reduce antagonisms within the community in this specific context, while admitting divergent contentions on other topics among the same population.

Because of the profile of exclusion, micro-insurance – which is designed to service excluded populations – must be sensitive to three conditions:

- it needs to be simple,
- it needs to be affordable and
- it needs to be accessible to members.

Unit 2: Main Features

Simplicity

Most people in the informal sector are unable to cope with procedural complexities. Many people simply cannot read or write and even literate persons might find it very difficult to "fill in the form" – for example because they may be unable to provide such seemingly simple details as an address, date of birth or information about their income. Formalities and procedures must take account of this reality.

Simplicity is important not only because of the technical problems. It projects a public image that micro-insurance is approachable by poor people. For the same reason, micro-insurance units have to be prepared to deal with applicants who join when they are in need, expecting immediate support, if for no other reason than that it is easiest to see the utility of insurance in moments of need. Response time on applications for affiliation must therefore be as short as possible. However, expeditious decisions about *induction* should not be confused with a decision to provide *immediate financial help*; micro-insurance units may have to impose some restrictions, particularly on expenses that are not random at the time of entry.

Another aspect of simplicity is to forgo recourse to mechanisms of exclusion. Commercial health insurance frequently excludes "prior medical conditions" from coverage – and for as long a period as possible. This is impractical with micro-insurance because of the cost involved in determining such exclusions.

Affordability

What makes micro-insurance affordable?

- The *absolute level of premiums* obviously makes a difference. Affordability is linked, at least partly, to a sense of utility.

- The *perceived return for the premium* can be as important as its absolute level. Also the feeling of confidence that, in case of need, the insurance will pay for the member enhances the subjective feeling of affordability.

- *Transparency* is a feature relevant to expenditure in general and overhead costs in particular. People tend to view as "affordable", costs which they feel are justified. Streamlining operations to reduce costs is as important in micro-insurance as it is in micro-finance or in any other financial activities which are oriented towards the poor.

- A further aspect of affordability is the *periodicity* of payment.

  Regular periodicity of income flow, characteristic of wage earners in the formal sector, is relatively rare with most people in rural or informal activity. People whose income periodicity is erratic cannot be expected to pay a regular monthly premium. Micro-insurance needs to be flexible enough to enable its affiliates to pay when they can. Similarly, the knowledge that all members have to abide by the same equitable rules is important.

- Finally, affordability may also depend on the *type of transaction* that is acceptable as payment. Some may have difficulty paying in cash but may have little or no difficulty paying in kind or by providing their labour. The community should therefore seek ways to accept payment in kind in cases where cash payment is problematic. This is plausible if micro-insurance units operate as extensions to other communal efforts (for example sale of agricultural crops) or if the insurance recruits staff from among the local community to perform administrative tasks related to micro-insurance, at low operating costs.

Proximity

Micro-insurance units need to be near their client base, simply because the poor or the rural population may have neither the means nor the capacity to travel from their place of residence to service centres. If micro-insurance units are to be started in a large locality, they might be more successful if launched in several sub-sectors of the larger community. In fact proximity is necessary throughout the operation, not only at recruitment, since the locus of decisions and the place where services are needed rests with the community.

Self management

In addition to the main characteristics of micro-insurance which have already been mentioned, another fundamental feature is its community base. *Micro-insurance is the enterprise of the community.* The democratic process of jointly defining the risks that should be covered is, in itself, unique to micro-insurance. Unlike *commercial* insurance (where the *insurer* determines the offer of insurance) or social health insurance (where the *government* determines the benefit package) *micro-insurance* depends on needs-based decision-making by the *beneficiaries* and is capped by the resources which *they* can commit. This approach provides several concurrent advantages.

- First, it enables the identification of priorities and fixes the qualifying conditions through participation of all. Admittedly, democratic participation in defining health risks may present some problems – notably access to medical knowledge which will have to come from outside (although health workers – nurses, midwives, first-aiders etc – have much health knowledge which should not be overlooked or denigrated). However, it is assumed that the community can define random catastrophic risks that are most feared by the members, as this category of risks will probably not be established solely on medical grounds.

A different logic may apply in respect of setting the priorities for health promotion, preventive and primary care. Prevention is effective when accidents occur, as they represent a tangible signal that something more serious can happen and people needy of first aid are sensitized to prevent the risk. This approach may open up avenues for collaboration between the micro-insurance unit and the agencies which deal with prevention or health promotion, who can provide technical expertise and funding.

- Secondly, autonomous decision-making enables a group of people to act as a cohesive social unit which can fulfill a role that no-one else can do better – that is to relate needs and priorities to their prevalent activity, to location-specific conditions and to the level of resources, etc..

- Thirdly, retaining decision-making powers within the community empowers it to control the flow of its funds. Two examples can illustrate this point:

    - the micro-insurance unit can change the benefit package rapidly, without the need to receive approval from the outside

    and

    - it can represent its members in negotiations with interlocutors outside, notably with providers.

Because micro-insurance services the poor, each unit must be particularly sensitive to keeping overheads low. All known alternatives to self-management, be they commercial or public, favour highly trained and expensive professional management, as is typical in the formal health sector. Replicating such a managerial profile seems incompatible not only with the sizes and quantities that need to be managed at the level of a single community but also with the kind of services that will be provided. *Self-management is thus not only a cost saving but also a right-sizing measure.*

Setting up micro-insurance units requires a relatively small nucleus of people and very little capital or infrastructure to start operations. There is no impediment to enlarging the group over time – both within the community and across communities. And the **triple autonomy**, whereby each micro-insurance unit defines its own insurable risk, organises financing of the insurance, and exercises control over the flow and management of its funds, provides a very potent formula.

Unit 3: Micro-Insurance as an alternative

One of the innovative features of micro-insurance is that it introduces a complex financial concept – health insurance – as an extension to familiar social interactions. This opens the door to improved contacts between excluded populations and financial markets, who frequently ignore the needs of poor and rural populations on the assumption that they are unable to pay for health services. Also, poor and rural people do not have the habit or the possibility of initiating individual negotiations to tailor insurance products to their conditions. The community, if helped and empowered, can serve both as an organizer of local self-help (as an alternative to the unavailable public help) and as a mediator between its membership and actors outside the community (such as public authorities – including providers of health services) or financial institutions.

The concept of micro-insurance presented in this module is based not only on theory but on some experience. A recent synthesis of 22 case studies (from 50 test communities) has this to say about the viability of the concept[12]:

"... Even now, they make a significant contribution to health care access and extending social protection to disadvantaged sections of the population by mainly targeting people in the informal and rural sectors. This also represents a contribution to equity in health care in the areas where they are active. Another area in which MHOs make a new – and in this case, original – contribution is that of democratic governance in the health sector... [and] in representing their communities or members before the health authorities in order to articulate the views of the consumers of health care. This gives them some weight in influencing the priorities, resource allocation decisions, and responsiveness of the health authorities to the concerns of the public on such issues as waiting times, staff behaviour, quality of services etc. This is a genuinely new contribution which reflects the role and origins of the MHOs as part of the growing and confident civic society that began to develop in Africa in the 1990s".

---

12 **Atim, Chris.** 1998. *The contribution of mutual health organizations to financing, delivery, and access to health care in West and Central Africa : Synthesis of research in nine countries.* Washington, PHR-USAID.

In short, the local level, the personal acquaintance of the membership with each other, the transparency of decisions, the autonomous low-cost management and the non-profit character of micro-insurance units are all amplifiers of social cohesion. The reliance of micro-insurance on the dynamics of social cohesion within the community is more than tactical; it is the strategy to seek acceptance of the concept of social health insurance among those who most need it.

EPILOGUE

Among the international agencies of the united nations family, technical competence for social security matters – *including health insurance* – is attributed to the International Labour Organization (ILO).

Standard setting, research, technical cooperation, training, and the dissemination of information on social security have been undertaken by the ILO for almost 80 years and ILO expertise in planning, implementing and financing health insurance schemes has been put at the disposal of a large number of countries and large financial institutions. Systems of delivering health care, financing concepts, and legislation have been applied and tested, in particular those which suit the conditions of developing countries.

On many occasions, these activities have been jointly undertaken with the World Health Organization (WHO), since both organizations – WHO and ILO – share the same common objectives and concerns.

There is a widespread desire, expressed by health policy planners and administrators, to explore the potential role of social security as a means of broadening the access of the population to primary health care and related health facilities and services.

The compulsory health insurance approach has, at times, been examined with some hesitation in Health Ministries and inadequate understanding – or misunderstandings – of the health insurance concept has sometimes resulted in its being seen as a threat ..... as though health insurance within the social security framework would take health care out of the domain of the Ministry of Health.

Thus there is a need for clarification and increased understanding of the *positive* aspects of social security – as well as its potential shortcomings – in the light of actual experience. It is hoped that, in the limited space available in this Manual, it has been possible to provide some of that clarification and to remove some of the misunderstanding.

Experience gained by the ILO shows that social security health insurance programmes can take a variety of forms – particularly with regard to

- the institutional framework
- the organization and delivery of health services

- relations with the medical profession
- financing.

It also needs to be remembered that, in most countries, there will exist three parallel schemes – social health insurance, the public health organization and private, "out of pocket" or "user charge" schemes.

The relationship and interplay between those schemes will have a number of consequences, and provide a number of challenges, for example:

- the necessity to produce equilibrium between:
- the three levels of care,
- provision in rural and urban areas,
- quantity, price and quality of care;
- how to limit tertiary care provision to no more than 5% of global health care expenditure;
- simultaneously, to valorize the functions of primary care providers, both in terms of revenues and services available to scheme members;
- clarifying the concept of "specialist/generalist" – perhaps by defining the minimum parameters of the health package and the health priorities to be provided;
- simultaneously reinforcing centralized functions (e.g. accounting and computerization) and decentralized functions (e.g. provider and risk management).

It is hoped that the manual will have made it apparent that there are wide areas for negotiation between the exclusive responsibilities of the state on the one hand and the social health insurance organization on the other. There is a variety of issues and topics which are crucial for the effectiveness, efficiency and maintenance of the health system and it is important to ensure that, within a country, these are fully debated *before*, not after, the introduction of a social health insurance scheme.

✱✱✱✱✱✱✱✱✱✱✱

The manual began by making clear that there is no one, single, standard model of social health insurance and any reader who had nevertheless hoped to find in these pages a description of such a model will have been disappointed for – as should already have become apparent in the preceding pages – there is no such thing!

FURTHER READING

Backaus J (ed.)
Health policy: international and historical dimensions
London, JAI Press Ltd, 1996, 380 p.
(International review of comparative policy, No. 6)
ISBN 1-55939-878-1

Cichon M, Gillion C (ILO)
Financing of health care in developing countries
International Labour Review 132(2), 1993, 173-186

Dror, D; Jaquier, Ch:
Micro-Insurance. Extending Health Insurance to the Excluded
International Social Security Review, ISSA, Vol. 52, No. 1,
January-March 1999 P. 71-97.

Figueras J, Tragakes E
(World Health Organization. Regional Office for Europe)
Health care systems in transition: production template and questionnaire
Copenhagen, WHO, 1996, 32 p.
(HiT profiles)

Hanmer L
(Institute of Social Studies, The Hague)
Equity and gender issues in health care provision: the 1993 World Bank Development Report and its implications for health service recipients
The Hague, 1994, 37 p.
(Working paper series, no. 172)

Huang PC, Lin RS, Chow LP
Health care in the changing economic and social environment
Greenwich CO, JAI Press, 1993, 410 p.
(Research in human capital and development, no. 7)
ISBN 1-55938-132-9

International Labour Office
Health care in developing countries: quality and cost-effectiveness
World Labour Report (7), 1994, p. 67-77 and 92-93
ISBN 92-2-108009-9

International Labour Office, Geneva
Introduction to social security
ISBN 92-2-103638-3

International Labour Office
Social security: a workers' education guide
Geneva, ILO, 1992, 113 p.
ISBN 92-2-108004-8

Koivusalo M, Ollila E
Making a healthy world: agencies, actors and policies in international health
London, Zen Books Ltd, 1997, 270 p.
ISBN 1-85649-493-4

Marrée J, Groenewegen P (eds.)
Back to Bismarck: Eastern Europe health care systems in transition
Aldershot, Ashgate Publishing Ltd, 1997, 137 p.
ISBN 1-85972-617-8

Normand C (World Health Organization), Weber A (ILO)
Social health insurance: a guidebook for planning
Geneva, WHO, 1994, 144 p.
(WHO--SHS/NHP/94.3)

Organization for Economic Cooperation and Development
OECD Health Systems
Paris, OECD, 1993. 2 vol.
(Health Policy Studies, no. 3)
(Vol. 1: Facts and trends, 1960-1991;
Vol. 2: Socio-economic environment statistical references)
ISBN 92-64-13800-5

Organization for Economic Cooperation and Development
Reform of the health care systems: a review of seventeen OECD countries
Paris, OECD, 1994, 340 p.
(Health policy studies, no. 5)
ISBN 92-64-14250-9

Organization for Economic Cooperation and Development
Health care reform: the will to change
Paris, 1996, 136 p.
(Health policy studies, no. 8 109210-0

Ron A, Abel-Smith B, Tamburi G (ILO)
Health insurance in developing countries: the social security approach
Geneva, ILO, 1990, 241p.
(Reprinted 1993; also published by Oxford &
IBH Publishing Co.Pvt.Ltd, New Delhi)
IBN 92-2-106475-1

Ron A
(ILO South-East Asia and the Pacific Multidisciplinary Advisory Team, Manila)
Health care in Asia and the Pacific: increasing the focus on social health insurance
International Social Security Review 51(2), 1998, 17-37

Scheil-Adlung X
(International Social Security Association)
Steering the health care ship: effects of market incentives to control costs in selected OECD countries
International Social Security Review 51(1), 1998, 103-136

Social Security Department, ILO Geneva
Health care under social security in Africa: Taking stock of experience and potential
ISBN 92-2-MODULE 5

Taylor SS
(Bureau of National Affairs, Washington)
Negotiating health insurance in the workplace: a basic guide
Washington, BNA, 1992, 346 p.
ISBN 0-87179-731-3

United States. Department of Health and Human Services. Social Security Administration
Social security programs throughout the world, 1997
Washington DC, SSA, 1997, 444 p.
(Research report, no. 65)

Youngman I
The health insurance opportunity: a worldwide study of private medical insurance markets
Dublin, Lafferty Publ., 1996, 212 p. ISBN 0-948394-96-X

NEW LITERATURE

Readers interested in keeping abreast of new literature may wish to consult the ILO's abstracting bulletin *International Labour Documentation*, under the heading Social Security, or read the regular Books section of the *International Social Security Review* issued by ISSA, or request data base searches from either of the following addresses:

Social Security Documentation Unit (SEC SOC/DOC),
International Labour Office,
CH-1211 Geneva 22, Switzerland.
Fax: + 41 22.799.7962
E-mail: SECSOC@ilo.org

International Social Security Documentation Centre (AISS/DOC),
International Social Security Association,
Case postale 1, CH-1211 Geneva 22, Switzerland.
Fax: + 41 22.799.8509
E-mail: Issadoc@ilo.org

ILO publications and documents can be ordered from

ILO Publications, CH-1211 Geneva 22, Switzerland.

For **ISSA publications and documents**, contact

ISSA Publications, cp 1, CH-1211 Geneva 22, Switzerland.

www.ingramcontent.com/pod-product-compliance
Ingram Content Group UK Ltd.
Pitfield, Milton Keynes, MK11 3LW, UK
UKHW051524180426
11947UKWH00018B/1564